SO YOU THINK YOU'RE A
CLEVELAND INDIANS
FAN?

STARS, STATS, RECORDS, AND MEMORIES FOR TRUE DIEHARDS

JOSEPH WANCHO

Visit our website at www.sportspubbooks.com.

10 9 8 7 6 5 4 3 2 1

Library of Congress Cataloging-in-Publication Data is available on file.

Cover design by Tom Lau
Cover photo credit: Associated Press

ISBN: 978-1-68358-219-9
Ebook ISBN: 978-1-68358-220-5

Printed in the United States of America

This book is dedicated to all Tribe fans
Young or old
Diehard or casual
Hopeful or pessimistic
Far and near

Contents

Introduction

Trivia—unimportant matters: trivial facts or details; also singular in construction: a quizzing game involving obscure facts—Merriam-Webster Dictionary.

Merriam-Webster penned the ideal definition of the word *trivia*. It is believed that it first came to be used in 1920. Of course, it was sixty years later with the creation of *Trivial Pursuit* that "trivia" became a national phenomenon. You saw trivia contests everywhere: magazines, newspapers, radio call-in shows, classrooms, college campuses. It was a new way to prove how knowledgeable one was.

The world of sports, with its players, teams, games, statistics, and stadiums, lends itself as the perfect vehicle for trivia. As much as sports is a part of the lives of so many, most would agree that compared to everyday life, the facts or details regarding sports are indeed "unimportant matters" as Merriam-Webster suggest. But the importance of trivia is certainly subjective.

And, of course, it's not an obscure fact if you know the answer to the question. Everybody has their own level of retention. I would guess that of the following questions, I knew the answers to about eighty of them. I am no trivia expert, but being a Tribe fan for over forty years, you hear bits and pieces of Indians and baseball history. Although my ego always goes up if I am watching *Jeopardy* and one of the categories is baseball. I run the table. Now give me something like US Presidents, and I will struggle.

I remember driving to work one day not so long ago, and the classic rock station I was listening to had a trivia contest in which the prize was a pair of tickets to an Indians game. The question was, "In the song 'Paradise by the Dashboard Light' by Meat Loaf, who was the baseball announcer that was providing the play-by-play sequence?'" As I was driving along, I was screaming at my radio "Phil Rizzuto! Phil Rizzuto!" The first caller obviously phoned in without knowing the answer, and he quickly hung up. The second caller had jumped the gun as well and was stumped by the question. With time running out, he blurted out "Herb Score." Herb Score? I just could not picture the well-mannered Score spending a day in a recording studio with Meat Loaf, not to mention talking as fast as Rizzuto does in his part of the song. To me, this is a perfect example of trivia.

As I went through the various resources looking for possible questions, my goal was to find a variety that spanned the last century or so of Cleveland baseball. I included questions about the postseason, All-Star Games, historic individual accomplishments, award recipients, trades, Hall of Famers, and, of course, the obscure.

You will notice that the questions are divided into four sections: Rookie, Starting Lineup, All-Star, and Hall of Fame. The easiest questions begin at the Rookie Level and are intended to get a bit more complex as you make your way through the book. The question and answers are designed to challenge and inform you. Most of the questions have comprehensive answers that contain informative data.

I hope you enjoy this journey through Tribe history. In spite of the franchise's lack of world championships and some rather dreary decades, there have been many memorable moments.

It is my pleasure to present it to you.

Roll Tribe!!

Joseph Wancho
Westlake, Ohio

1
ROOKIE LEVEL

ROOKIE LEVEL

(Answers begin on page 7)

1. Which Cleveland Indians players have been selected as American League Rookie of the Year by both the Baseball Writers' Association of America and *The Sporting News*?

2. Who was the Cleveland Naps player that was born in Bedford, Ohio, batted a career .313, and was elected to the Hall of Fame in 1963?

3. The Cleveland Indians have had only one player who was named Most Valuable Player of an All-Star Game. Who was he?

4. The Cleveland Indians have had four pitchers who have been selected as an American League Cy Young Award winner. Who are these four pitchers?

5. Who is the all-time club leader in home runs, walks, and strikeouts for the Indians?

6. On June 10, 1959, which Tribe slugger hit four home runs in one game at Baltimore's Memorial Stadium?

7. Which National League player had two home runs in the 1981 All-Star Game held at Cleveland Stadium?

8. Which Indians player hit two home runs in the same inning, one from each side of the plate? He was the first to do it in major-league history.

9. The only pitcher in major league history to win 500 or more games won his 500th in a Cleveland uniform. It

3

happened on July 19, 1910, at American League Park in Washington. Who was this all-time great?

10. Beginning in 1983, the Baseball Writers' Association of America has selected a Manager of the Year for each league. Two Cleveland Indians managers have been chosen for this honor. Who are the two skippers in this exclusive club?

11. In Game Six of the 1997 American League Championship Series, which Cleveland Indians player homered in the top of the 11th inning at Camden Yards to eventually give the Indians a 1–0 victory over the Orioles and the pennant?

12. Which Cleveland Indian has been selected for the most Gold Glove Awards in team history?

13. Which Cleveland Indians player was selected to the most All-Star Games in team history?

14. On August 5, 2001, at Jacobs Field, the Cleveland Indians came back from a 12-run deficit to defeat which team?

15. On July 1, 2016, the Cleveland Indians set a then-franchise record by winning 14 games in a row. The game, which was played at the Rogers Centre, went 19 innings as the Tribe beat Toronto, 2–1. Which player smacked a home run in the top of the 19th inning?

16. Not counting #42 that was retired to honor Jackie Robinson, the Cleveland Indians have honored seven players by retiring their uniform number. Who are these seven immortals?

17. Babe Ruth made his major-league debut on July 11, 1914, against the Cleveland Naps at Fenway Park. Who was the first Cleveland batter Ruth faced and who later

went on to become one of the first broadcasters in the big leagues?

18. Cleveland general manager Frank Lane and Detroit GM Bill DeWitt swapped managers on August 3, 1960. Who were the two field managers involved in the deal?

19. Which Cleveland Indian was the first African American player to hit a home run in a World Series?

20. On May 15, 1981, Len Barker threw a perfect game, defeating the Toronto Blue Jays, 3–0. Which member of the Blue Jays left the major leagues after that season and pursued a basketball career in the NBA?

21. What Cleveland slugger is the only player in major-league history to hit at least 50 home runs and 50 doubles in the same season?

22. What is the only defensive position that Cleveland has never had a Gold Glove winner?

23. During their 2016 postseason run, which Cleveland Indian had the most home runs with four?

24. On August 16, 1920, the Cleveland Indians suffered a tragic loss when shortstop Ray Chapman was hit in the head by the Yankees' Carl Mays. Chapman died hours later from the impact of the baseball fracturing his skull. Who was the player that stepped into the shortstop position that season and subsequently was elected to the Hall of Fame in 1977?

25. On July 24, 1911, a charity game was held at League Park with the proceeds being turned over to the family of what Cleveland pitcher, who passed away at the age of thirty-one from tubercular meningitis on April 14, 1911?

ROOKIE LEVEL — ANSWERS

1. Cleveland has had four players so honored as the league's top rookie. The quartet includes Herb Score (1955), Chris Chambliss (1971), Joe Charboneau (1980), and Sandy Alomar Jr. (1990).

Herb Score burst onto the scene after being named Minor League Player of the Year by *The Sporting News* in 1954. The tall left-hander posted a 22–5 record for the Indianapolis Indians of the American Association. He set a league record of 330 strikeouts over 251 innings. Score added a changeup to pair with his lethal fastball when he arrived in Cleveland in 1955, and he set a new record for strikeouts among rookie pitchers with 245. The previous mark of 227 was set by the Phillies' Grover Cleveland Alexander in 1911. His overall record was 16–10 with a 2.85 ERA. He was named to the AL All-Star team by Indians manager Al Lopez. In his typical self-deprecating manner, Score said "I was surprised being chosen for *The Sporting News* rookie award. I thought of several others who were more deserving. I guess I got it because of my strikeout record." Dwight Gooden of the New York Mets would shatter Score's rookie mark by posting 276 strikeouts in 1984.

In only his fourth start of his big-league career on May 1, 1955, Score struck out 16 batters in a 2–1 victory over the Red Sox. Score became the tenth pitcher to strike out 16 or more batters since 1900. This performance by Score was the second game of a doubleheader. In the opener, Bob Feller defeated

Herb Score's career was cut short by a batted ball that struck his right eye on May 7, 1957. He returned to pitching but was never the same. After his playing career, Score was a Tribe broadcaster, first on TV, then radio from 1964 to 1997. According to broadcast partner Joe Tait, "Herb Score has probably watched more bad baseball than anyone in the history of the game."
Courtesy of Cleveland Public Library/Photograph Collection.

Boston by a score of 2–0. It was the 12th one-hitter that Feller threw in his incomparable career.

Chris Chambliss was selected by Cleveland with the first overall pick in the January 1970 amateur draft. Chambliss reported to Wichita of the American Association and was named the league's Rookie of the Year after leading the circuit with a .342 batting average in 1970. Ken Harrelson was the Tribe's starting first baseman in 1971, attempting to come back from a leg injury the previous season. Chambliss was returned to Wichita when he suffered a right thigh muscle injury in spring training. At Wichita, Chambliss was involved in a collision at home plate. After further examination, the muscle was diagnosed as being ruptured. He returned to Cleveland for rehab, eventually joining the Indians on May 17. Chambliss made his major-league debut on May 28 and promptly got a hit in 14 of his first 16 games. Harrelson retired shortly thereafter. For the year, Chambliss batted .275 with nine home runs and 48 RBIs. He had 114 hits in 111 games. In 404 games in a Tribe uniform, Chambliss batted .282 with 26 home runs and 152 RBIs.

Chambliss played for 17 years in the major leagues. He made stops in Cleveland, with the New York Yankees, and with Atlanta. He was part of three pennant winners with the Yankees and two world championships. He won the Gold Glove in 1978 for his excellent fielding ability at first base.

After being drafted by Philadelphia in 1976, **Joe Charboneau** was dealt to Cleveland in 1978. He batted a league-leading .352 at Class AA Chattanooga of the Southern League in 1979. In 1980, Charboneau became a folk hero of sorts in Cleveland for his home runs and the bizarre stories he would tell. Charboneau admitted that many of the tales that he spoke of were fabrications or just not true. He was given the nickname "Super Joe," and on one night in particular, he lived up to the moniker. On June 28, 1980, Charboneau smashed a solo home run off New York's Tom Underwood. The baseball kept rising and rising until it reached the third deck at Yankee Stadium. Although the Indians lost, 11–10, that evening, the legend grew. "I remember it like it was yesterday," Charboneau recounted years later. "As I was going around second base, I looked up to where the ball landed and thought to myself that I'd probably never hit another ball like that again. And I never did."

Comparisons between Charboneau and Rocky Colavito began to be the talk at corner bars. For the year, Charboneau batted .289 with 23 home runs and 87 RBIs. Unfortunately, a back injury the following year curtailed Charboneau's career. He only hit six more home runs after his rookie season. His final game in the majors was on June 1, 1982.

Sandy Alomar Jr. comes from a baseball family. His father, Sandy Sr., was a 15-year veteran in the major leagues, primarily as an infielder. Sandy's brother Roberto was one of the elite second baseman in major-league history. Roberto's 17-year career ended with two world championships, 12 All-Star Games, 10 Gold Gloves, and election into the Hall of Fame in 2011.

Sandy followed his brother by signing with the San Diego Padres. He was named *The Sporting News* Minor League Player of the Year in both 1988 and 1989. But Alomar was a catcher, and the Padres already had an established backstop in Benito Santiago. On December 6, 1989, Alomar was traded with Carlos Baerga and Chris James to Cleveland for Joe Carter. Alomar was given the starting job and batted .290 with nine home runs and 66 RBIs. He was selected as the AL starting catcher for the 1990 All-Star Game at Wrigley Field in Chicago. He was also the recipient of the Gold Glove.

Like his father and brother, Alomar had a long career. He played mostly for Cleveland and the Chicago White Sox in his 20-year career, which included six All-Star Games.

2. Elmer Flick is the pride of Bedford, Ohio, a southeastern suburb of Cleveland. Flick was playing semipro ball for Dayton in the Interstate League in 1897 when Philadelphia Phillies manager George Stallings spotted him. Stallings signed Flick to a contract for the 1898 season, and he was a member of the Phillies for four years. In 1900, Flick batted .367 and led the circuit with 110 RBIs.

In 1902, he jumped to the Philadelphia Athletics of the AL and subsequently joined Cleveland. He led the league in triples three consecutive years (1905–07) and in stolen bases (1904, 1906). His batting average of .308 led the loop in 1905. Flick's last season with the Naps and in the big leagues was 1910. A gastrointestinal illness cut his career short. In 13 seasons, he batted .313, stole 330 bases, and scored 950 runs. In 1907, Detroit offered to trade Ty Cobb straight up for Flick, but Cleveland refused any overtures.

Flick was selected by the Veteran's Committee for enshrinement into the Hall of Fame in 1963. His career was forgotten by many, but when Cobb passed away in 1961, the stories about the potential Cobb-Flick trade surfaced. It caused many to take another look as to what kind of career Flick actually had.

On September 25, 2013, the city of Bedford honored Flick with a ceremony and the unveiling of a bronze statue of Flick in its town square. The two-hour ceremony was attended by representatives of the Cleveland Indians, including Mike Hargrove, Len Barker, Joe Charboneau, and front office executive Bob DiBiasio.

3. As of 2017, Sandy Alomar Jr. is the only Indians player to be named MVP of the midsummer classic. On July 8, 1997, the 68th All-Star Game was held at Jacobs Field in Cleveland. The game was uncharacteristically low-scoring, as the AL and

NL battled to a 1–1 tie heading into the bottom of the seventh inning. Each run came as the result of a solo home run as Seattle's Edgar Martínez and Atlanta's Javy López went yard.

Bernie Williams of the New York Yankees walked with one out and went to second base on a wild pitch by Shawn Estes of San Francisco. Alomar stepped to the plate and sent a 2-2 offering from Estes to the bleachers in left field. The blast was the final margin of victory for the AL, 3–1. "I felt like I was flying," said Alomar. "I've never run the bases so fast on a home run."

It was quite a year for Alomar. The veteran backstop started the season in fine fashion, as he slugged a home run in five consecutive games from April 4-8. He owned the second-longest hitting streak in franchise history, 30 games, from May 25 through July 6. Alomar batted .422 during the streak. "It's been a remarkable run for him," said the Twins' Paul Molitor. "To be able to have the mind-set to call a game [as catcher] and still be able to do that . . ."

It was Alomar's fifth All-Star Game appearance in his career. "This is a dream I don't want to wake up from," said Alomar. "You probably only get one chance to play an All-Star Game in your home stadium." He was the first player to be honored with the ASG MVP in his home park.

4. As of 2017, Gaylord Perry, CC Sabathia, Cliff Lee, and Corey Kluber are the four Cleveland pitchers who have been honored as the American League's finest hurler. Kluber is the only Cleveland pitcher to win the award twice.

Former baseball commissioner Ford Frick is credited with establishing the Cy Young Award to honor baseball's greatest hurler, Cy Young. The first recipient was named in 1956, one year after Young had passed away. The award was initially awarded to the top pitcher in the major leagues. But after Frick retired in 1965, the decision was made to honor the top pitcher in each league beginning with the 1967 season.

Gaylord Perry won the award in 1972, his first season in the American League. Perry was traded from San Francisco to Cleveland along with shortstop Frank Duffy for pitcher Sam McDowell. Perry posted a 24–16 record with a 1.92 ERA. His 24 wins tied Wilbur Wood of Chicago for the league best, while he led the circuit in complete games with 29. His ERA ranked second, and he was third in strikeouts with 234. He was especially tough on opposing teams in May (6–1, 1.61 ERA), July (5–1, 1.07), and September (4–2, 1.04).

Perry received nine first place votes and 64 total points. He edged out Wood, who received seven first place votes and 58 total points. "The guy I owe this award to the most is [Cleveland catcher] Ray Fosse," said Perry. "He kept pushing me in games where I didn't have good stuff. I'd have to compare Fosse with Tom Haller, my catcher with the Giants. And I have great respect for Haller."

The only month that Perry hit a rough patch was in August (2–6, 3.83). "That was when I was shaking off Ray's signs," said Perry. "If you get away from the pattern he sets up for you, that's when you get your ears pinned back. You look for early showers."

Jim Perry, Gaylord's older brother, won the Cy Young award in 1970 as a member of the Minnesota Twins. They are the only brother duo to each win the award. In 1978, Gaylord won the award again while he was a member of the San Diego Padres (21–6, 2.73 ERA). He is one of only five pitchers in major-league history to win the award in each league (Pedro

Martínez, Roger Clemens, Roy Halladay, and Max Scherzer are the others).

CC Sabathia was the second Indians pitcher to win the Cy Young Award. Sabathia went 19–7 with a 3.21 ERA in 2007. He received 19 first-place votes for a total of 119 total points. Boston's Josh Beckett was the runner-up with eight first-place votes and 86 points overall. "It means a lot," said Sabathia. "I hadn't really had a chance to sit down and think about it yet. You guys know how I am about numbers and thinking about individual awards. It feels good right now. I can't really put it into words, but I'm sure later on tonight when I have a chance to sit down with my family and think about it, I'll have some words for it. But right now, I'm just happy that it happened this year."

Sabathia was selected by Cleveland with their first pick in the first round (20th overall) of the 1998 amateur draft. He made his major-league debut in 2001 and went 17–5. He was named American League Rookie Pitcher of the Year by *The Sporting News* in 2001. In eight years with Cleveland, Sabathia was 106–71 with a 3.83 ERA. He totaled 1,265 strikeouts.

The big lefty was traded to Milwaukee in 2008 (his contract year) as the Indians were losing and looking to rebuild their roster. Sabathia (11–2, 1.65 ERA) led the Brewers to their first playoff appearance since 1982.

In the offseason, Sabathia signed with the New York Yankees. He led the American League in wins in 2009 (19) and 2010 (21). In 2009, the Yankees won the World Series, defeating the Philadelphia Phillies in six games.

Cliff Lee made it two years in a row that a Cy Young Award winner wore an Indians uniform. With Sabathia on the trading block, Lee became the top starter and responded with a

22–3 record and a 2.54 ERA. Lee led the AL in wins and ERA. It was the first time an Indians pitcher won 20 or more games in a season since Gaylord Perry won 21 in 1974.

Lee was selected by Montreal in the fourth round of the amateur draft on June 5, 2000. He was traded along with Grady Sizemore, Brandon Phillips, and Lee Stevens to Cleveland for pitchers Bartolo Colón and Tim Drew on June 27, 2002.

He made his major-league debut the same year. He posted an 18–5 record in 2005 and 14–11 in 2006, but Lee couldn't keep his spot in the rotation in 2007. He was demoted to Class AAA Buffalo of the International League.

Lee won his first six decisions in 2008 and won eight consecutive games from August 4 to September 12. The Indians dealt him at the 2009 trade deadline as they had with Sabathia the previous season. Lee went to Philadelphia and pitched well for the Phillies, going 7–4 with a 3.39 ERA. Philadelphia won the National League pennant, and the Phillies faced the Yankees in the World Series. The Game One matchup featured CC Sabathia vs. Cliff Lee. The Phillies won by a score of 6–1, but the Yankees won the series in six games. Lee won both games for the Phillies.

Lee retired in 2014, having also pitched for Seattle and Texas. In 13 seasons, Lee was 143–91 with a 3.52 ERA. In eight seasons with Cleveland, Lee's record was 83–48 with a 4.01 ERA and 826 strikeouts.

Corey Kluber was the Tribe's fourth recipient of the Cy Young Award. He captured the honor in 2014 after posting an 18–9 record with a 2.44 ERA and 269 strikeouts. He received 17 first-place votes and 169 total points while runner-up Félix Hernández of Seattle tallied 13 first-place votes and 159 points. "I wasn't expecting it," said Kluber. "I definitely thought Félix was going to win. He had such a great year. To me, I guess I just assumed that who he is and how good of a year he had and all that kind of stuff would get him more votes . . . . I'm very appreciative of it. Obviously, I think it's one of those things where I would've been in no position to have any kind of argument if he would've won."

Kluber was again recognized as the AL Cy Young Award recipient in 2017. He was voted first on twenty-eight of thirty ballots. Kluber was 18–4 with a 2.25 ERA and 265 strikeouts. His ERA was the lowest in the major leagues.

San Diego drafted Kluber in the fourth round in 2007. Cleveland acquired Kluber on July 31, 2010, as part of a three-way deal with San Diego and St. Louis.

He made his major-league debut in 2011, but he did not become part of the Tribe rotation until 2013. Kluber responded with an 11–5 record and an ERA of 3.85. Justin Masterson was designated as the ace of the Indians staff in 2014. But he faltered badly and was traded to the Cardinals. Kluber took over the number one spot in the rotation and won the Cy Young Award.

Kluber led the AL in losses in 2015 with 16. Still, he pitched well enough to finish with a 3.49 ERA. He rebounded with a superb 2016 season. He went 18–9 with a 3.14 ERA. The Indians returned to the postseason, and Kluber posted a 4–1 record, including two wins in the World Series. He has totaled at least 227 strikeouts in each season from 2014 to 2017.

5. Jim Thome is the career leader in all three categories for the Cleveland Indians. Thome accumulated 337 home runs, 1,008 walks, and 1,400 strikeouts in 1,399 games played.

Cleveland drafted the Peoria, Illinois native in the 13th round in 1989. Thome made his major-league debut in 1991 and became the starting third baseman in 1994. When Cleveland acquired Matt Williams from San Francisco in November of 1996, Thome was moved to first base, where he was a mainstay for the next six seasons.

Thome was a fan favorite for his down-to-earth and unassuming personality. His home runs were not cheap ones, as they were often tape measure clouts. The left-handed power hitter would often show his strength by going the opposite way with his line drives. He was more than a home run hitter, as he hit over .270 in seven different seasons with the Indians.

Thome was an integral part of the Indians' pennant-winning teams in 1995 and 1997. He hit 17 home runs in six postseasons with Cleveland. In addition, Thome totaled 928 runs, 1,353 hits, 263 doubles, 937 RBIs, and batted .287 while with Cleveland.

In 2002, Thome was the recipient of the Roberto Clemente Award. The annual award that honors the Pittsburgh Pirates great is presented "to recognize a player who combines outstanding skill on the field with devoted work in the community." It was further testament to Thome's popularity in Cleveland.

In 2003, Thome signed on with Philadelphia and led the National League in home runs (47) and strikeouts (182). He returned to the American League in 2006 to play for the Chicago White Sox, his hometown team. For the rest of his career, because of injuries, Thome was relegated to the role of designated hitter.

On August 15, 2011, at Detroit's Comerica Park, Thome smashed his 599th and 600th career home runs while a member of the Minnesota Twins. He became the eighth person to achieve the monumental feat and the first player in major-league history to hit both homers in the same game. It was fitting that Thome hit the historic blast against the Tigers, as he had hit more home runs against Detroit (66) than any other club in his 22-year career.

"It's an unbelievable night. You dream about it, but when it happens, it's kind of surreal," said Thome. "You envision, is it ever going to happen? You don't know. At forty years old, approaching forty-one, you don't know. I never tried to take it for granted." Ten days later, he was sold to the Indians and finished his career in 2012 with the Phillies and Orioles.

In a career that spanned 22 years, he compiled 612 home runs, 1,699 RBIs, 451 doubles, 1,747 walks, a batting average of .276, and a slugging percentage of .554. He currently ranks eighth all-time in home runs and seventh in walks.

As of 2018, Thome works in the White Sox front office as a special assistant to senior vice president Rick Hahn. He is also an analyst with MLB.TV. In 2018, Thome became eligible for induction into the Hall of Fame, where he will one day take his place next to baseball's immortals.

6. Rocky Colavito was the Tribe player who was enjoying a personal home run derby in Baltimore. The Bronx, New York, native was a fan favorite. "Don't Knock the Rock" became a mantra of sorts for many of the little leaguers around Cleveland, Ohio, in the late 1950s. He had established himself as a legitimate star over his first couple of years in the league. In 1958, he smacked 41 home runs and drove in 113 runs. He led the league in slugging with a percentage of .620.

Perhaps it seemed a bit prophetic when *The Sporting News* ran an article entitled "Best Bet to Beat Bambino's 60?" in its June 10, 1959 issue. Colavito was named as the sure bet in the AL to surpass Babe Ruth's single-season home run mark. Eddie Mathews of Milwaukee was given the nod in the National League.

Against the Orioles, Colavito hit home runs in the third, fifth, sixth, and ninth innings. He totaled six RBIs and five runs scored in the Indians' 11–8 win. He became the eighth player in major-league history to hit four home runs in one game. Colavito was the third player in history to hit four home runs on consecutive at-bats. The other two players were Bobby Lowe of the 1894 Boston Beaneaters and Lou Gehrig of the New York Yankees in 1932. "Gehrig? No kidding," said Colavito. "He was my favorite player when I was a little kid. My brother, Vito, was a first baseman and he loved Gehrig; so naturally, I did, too." The Rock led the AL in home runs in 1959 with 42. He led the team in RBIs with 111.

Just before the 1960 season, Colavito was traded to Detroit for Harvey Kuenn. General manager Frank Lane was vilified by the Cleveland press corps, and of course, the Indians fans. Colavito belted 139 home runs over four seasons with the Tigers.

He eventually returned to Cleveland for the 1965 season, leading the league in RBIs with 108. But the Indians paid a price to reacquire the popular Colavito. Cleveland gave up outfielder Tommie Agee and pitcher Tommy John. Both players went on to have good careers after leaving the Indians. Colavito retired after the 1968 season, his 14th in the big leagues. He hit 374 home runs, drove in 1,159 runs, and batted .266 for his career.

Rocky Colavito was a feared right-handed batter who unfortunately spent his prime years in Detroit. Gabe Paul said of the Colavito trade for Harvey Kuenn: "The Indians traded a slow guy with power for a slow guy with no power." Paul reacquired Colavito after becoming the Indians' general manager.
Courtesy of the Cleveland Public Library/Photograph Collection.

7. Gary Carter of the Montreal Expos hit two solo home runs in the 52nd midsummer classic held at Cleveland Stadium on August 9, 1981.

Major League Baseball was hit by a player's strike on June 12, 1981. Games that were scheduled from June 12 through August 9 were cancelled and not made up. The season was divided into two halves. The division winners from the first half would play the winner of the second, thus creating an extra tier of playoffs. The second season commenced after the August 9 All-Star Game.

Carter, who was named Most Valuable Player of the game, clubbed his first home run in the top of the fifth inning off of Ken Forsch of California. His second home run was in the top of the seventh frame off of Ron Davis of the New York Yankees. On the day, Carter went 2-for-3 with two home runs, two RBIs, and two runs scored. It was Carter's fourth appearance in the All-Star Game, but his first as a starter. He was also named MVP of the 1984 All-Star Game at Candlestick Park in San Francisco, a 3–1 NL victory.

However, it took Philadelphia slugger Mike Schmidt's two-run smash in the top of the eighth inning to give the National League a 5–4 win. It was the senior circuit's tenth win in a row, and they captured their seventeenth win in the last eighteen games. A record All-Star Game crowd of 72,086 was in attendance.

8. Carlos Baerga entered the record books on April 8, 1993. He hit two home runs in the seventh inning against the New York Yankees, one from each side of the plate. He was batting right-handed when he connected off Steve Howe for a two run-shot, then hit a solo home run batting left-handed off of Steve Farr.

The Indians scored nine runs in the inning on their way to a 15–5 victory. "It's exciting," said Baerga. "They told me I set a record when I got back to the dugout after the second homer, but I didn't believe them. When I got to the clubhouse after the game, Bobby DiBiasio, our public-relations man, told me I'd set a record."

The San Diego Padres signed Baerga as an amateur free agent on November 4, 1985. Stuck behind Roberto Alomar in the Padres minor-league chain, Baerga was packaged together with Sandy Alomar Jr. and Chris James in a trade to Cleveland for Joe Carter on December 6, 1989.

Baerga played several infield positions his first two seasons. But he settled in at second base for good in 1992. Baerga had back-to-back seasons (1992–93) of batting .300 with at least 20 home runs, 200 hits, and 100 or more runs scored. He was the first second baseman to accomplish the feat since Rogers Hornsby turned the trick in 1921 and 1922.

Baerga was a key part to the Indians' pennant-winning club in 1995. However, the following year his production began to decline and in a surprising move, he was traded to the New York Mets as part of a four-player deal on July 29, 1996. However, the National League did not offer much of a respite for Baerga, and he could never return to his former level of production.

Baerga played for a number of teams after the Mets, even returning to Cleveland in 1999. In his 14-year career, Baerga totaled 1,583 hits, 134 home runs, 774 RBIs, 279 doubles, and batted .291.

Baerga is still a fan favorite in Cleveland. He serves as a baseball ambassador for the Indians and makes many public appearances. In 2016, Baerga threw out the first pitch of Game Two of the World Series at Progressive Field. He was, of course, cheered enthusiastically as he threw a perfect strike to home plate.

9. Denton True Young, better known as Cy Young, is the only pitcher to win 500 or more games, beating Washington, 5–2, for his 500th win while a member of the Cleveland Naps.

Pitching in the second game of a weekday doubleheader, Young was on the short end of a 1–0 game heading into the ninth inning. The Naps scored two runs in the top of the ninth inning via a walk, two bunt singles, and two sacrifice flies. But the Senators reached Young for one run in the bottom of the frame to knot the score at two. In the 11th inning, Cleveland loaded the bases with two walks and a scratch hit before a walk to catcher Ted Easterly forced in the go-ahead run. George Stovall followed with a hit to short left field to score two more runs, and the final margin.

Young, who was forty-three years of age, pitched all 11 innings, striking out three, walking three, and scattering four hits. He was in his 21st season of a 22-year career. He originally broke in with the Cleveland Spiders in 1890, where he played until 1898. He pitched for two years with the St. Louis Perfectos before moving on to join the Boston Americans of the new American League in 1901. Young won 30 or more games five times and won 20 or more games in fifteen seasons. In six seasons, Young's ERA was less than two runs.

Not only has Cy Young won the most games in major-league history with 511, he has also lost the most games, 316. He totaled 2,803 strikeouts in his career and had an ERA of 2.63.

10. Eric Wedge (2007) and Terry Francona (2013, 2016) have been the Indians' only two recipients of the Manager of the Year Award.

Eric Wedge was drafted in the third round by Boston in 1989. The Fort Wayne, Indiana, native had a great career at Wichita State. He was named Missouri Valley Conference Player of the Year in 1989 when he was a member of their national championship team. Wedge batted .380 with 23 homers and 99 RBIs. Wedge also had a 25-game hitting streak in 1989.

From 1989 through 1992 and again from 1994 to 1995, Wedge was a minor-league player at various levels for Boston. Wedge was selected in the 1992 expansion draft by the Colorado Rockies. Wedge spent 1993 with both the Rockies and their Class AAA affiliate in Colorado Springs.

Wedge did see some limited action with the Red Sox and the Rockies between 1991 and 1994. He appeared in 39 games with 86 at-bats and a .233 lifetime batting average.

Wedge was hired as the manager of Cleveland's low Class A Columbus Red Stixx in 1998. He progressed through the minor-league chain with much success. He was selected as the Carolina League Manager of the Year in 1999 after leading high Class A Kinston to a 79–58 record.

In 2001, Wedge led Triple-A Buffalo to the International League playoffs with a 91–51 record. *Baseball America* named him their Triple-A Manager of the Year. In 2002, the Bisons returned to the postseason with an 87–57 record, and *The Sporting News* tabbed Wedge as their Minor League Manager of the Year.

Cleveland and manager Charlie Manuel parted ways at the All-Star break in 2002. Wedge was hired to take over the

Tribe beginning in 2003. In 2005, Wedge led the Indians to a 92–69 record, but they were eliminated from playoff contention on the last weekend of the season.

In 2007, the Indians finished with a 96–66 record and won the American League Central Division for the first time since 2001. They eliminated the New York Yankees in four games in the League Division Series but lost to Boston in the ALCS in seven games.

The 2009 season was Wedge's last one in Cleveland. His record was 561–573 (.495). His 561 wins rank him fifth on the all-time list for Cleveland managers.

Wedge managed in Seattle from 2011 to 2013. He suffered a stroke in July 2013 and was idle for a portion of the season. He moved on to work at ESPN as a studio analyst from 2014–15. On February 6, 2016, Wedge was hired as a player development advisor for the Toronto Blue Jays.

Terry Francona is the son of Tito Francona, who was a first baseman and outfielder for the Indians from 1959 to 1964.

While he was a junior at the University of Arizona in 1980, Francona batted .401. He was awarded the Golden Spikes Award given annually to the nation's top amateur player. In the College World Series, won by the Wildcats, Francona batted .458 and was named College Player of the Year by *The Sporting News*.

Francona was drafted in the first round (22nd pick overall) that year by the Montreal Expos.

In a 10-year major-league career (1981–90), Francona played for Montreal, the Chicago Cubs, Cincinnati, Cleveland, and Milwaukee. He batted .274 in 708 at-bats for his career.

He started his managerial career in the minor leagues in 1992 with South Bend, the Chicago White Sox Single-A affiliate in the Midwest League. From 1993 to 1995 he managed their Double-A team, the Birmingham Barons of the Southern League. He led the Barons to a 78–64 record in 1993 and was named *Baseball America*'s Minor League Manager of the Year. The following year, Francona managed Michael Jordan, who briefly retired from the NBA to play baseball.

Francona served as Buddy Bell's third-base coach at Detroit in 1996 and then received his first managerial job in Philadelphia. His record with the Phillies was 285–363 from 1997 to 2000.

Boston hired Francona, and in seven seasons (2004–11), he compiled a 774–552 record and a .574 winning percentage. He led the Red Sox to five postseason appearances and two world championships (2004, 2007). Francona ranks second in Red Sox history in wins behind Joe Cronin (1,071). Francona and Bill Carrigan are the only managers in Red Sox history to lead Boston to multiple world championships.

Francona joined ESPN as a game analyst in 2012, and then accepted the Indians managerial job in 2013. He led them to a wild card in 2013 with a 92–70 record. In 2016, Cleveland won its first AL Central Division title since 2007 with a 94–67 record. Cleveland won its first pennant since 1997, giving Francona his third pennant in 13 years.

11. Tony Fernández hit a solo home run in the top of the 11th inning to give the Indians a 1–0 lead. José Mesa came in to close out the Orioles in the bottom of the inning to send the Indians to their second World Series in three years.

Fernández, who hails from the Dominican Republic, was signed by Toronto in 1979 as an amateur free agent. He quickly got the reputation as a smooth-fielding shortstop for the Blue

Jays as he won the American League Gold Glove Award each season from 1986 to 1989.

He was a key member of the Blue Jays, who won American League East Division titles in 1985 and 1989. However, a blockbuster deal was made with San Diego on December 5, 1990, when Fernández and first baseman Fred McGriff were sent to the Padres for second baseman Roberto Alomar and outfielder Joe Carter.

Two years later, Fernández was traded to the New York Mets. His stay was short, as on June 11, 1993, Fernández returned to Toronto via a trade as outfielder Darrin Jackson headed to New York. Fernández started 94 games for Toronto, batting .306 and fielding the shortstop position at a .985 clip. He formed a formidable keystone combo with second baseman Roberto Alomar, as the Blue Jays won their second straight world championship.

After stops with Cincinnati and the New York Yankees, the Indians signed Fernández on December 28, 1996. He had sat out the 1996 season with the Yankees after shattering his right elbow in spring training. Now he was coming to Cleveland to play second base and was paired with shortstop Omar Vizquel.

Fernández batted .286 for the Indians in 1997, hitting 11 home runs and driving in 44 runs. He appeared in 109 games at second base for the Indians, fielding .980. He also played in 10 games at shortstop.

Ironically, for all of his great fielding ability, it was an error by Fernández in Game Seven of the 1997 World Series that contributed to the Indians' loss. In the bottom of the 11th inning, the Marlins had a runner on second base and one out. Greg Counsell rolled a grounder to Fernández who saw the ball go through his legs and into right field. The error put runners on first and third with one out, and they eventually scored to win their first world championship.

12. Omar Vizquel has fielded the most Gold Glove Awards in franchise history with eight. Vizquel, who was a member of the Cleveland Indians from 1994 to 2004, won the Gold Glove for outstanding fielding at his shortstop position from 1994 to 2001. In addition, Vizquel won the award while with Seattle in 1993 and with San Francisco in 2005 and 2006. Vizquel's 11 total Gold Glove Awards for shortstops is second only to Ozzie Smith, who had 13 in his career.

Vizquel, a native of Caracas, Venezuela, was signed as an amateur free agent by the Seattle Mariners on April 1, 1984. Vizquel was assigned to Butte in the Pioneer League. He ascended through the Mariners chain, stopping at every level on his way up through the organization. Although he did not hit for average, Vizquel was an excellent fielder and showed a propensity for stealing bases as he totaled 25 in 1987 and 32 in 1988.

He made his major-league debut with Seattle on April 3, 1989. Except for a trip to the disabled list and subsequent rehab period in the minors in 1990, Vizquel was the Mariners' starting shortstop through 1993. He was traded to Cleveland after that season for shortstop Félix Fermín and first baseman Reggie Jefferson.

Vizquel's outgoing and pleasant personality made him an instant fan favorite in Cleveland. His barehanded grabs on groundballs and the wide range he showed at shortstop solidified him as a main cog in the Indians machine in the 1990s. He had a career-high 14 home runs and 72 RBIs in 2002. In 11 years with Cleveland, Vizquel played in 1,478 games, batted .283, and totaled 1,616 hits and 279 stolen bases.

Vizquel moved on to San Francisco in 2005 and won two more Gold Gloves. National League fans now got to see what the AL fans already knew—Omar Vizquel was a special baseball player.

He retired in 2012 after one year with Toronto. He totaled 2,877 hits in his career. In 2,709 games at shortstop, Vizquel's fielding percentage was .985.

From 2014 to 2017, Vizquel served as the Detroit Tigers' first-base coach. Vizquel managed his native Venezuela in the 2017 World Baseball Classic. He was hired on December 5, 2017 to manage the Winston-Salem Dash, the Chicago White Sox' Class A affiliate in the Carolina League.

13. Bob Feller has been named to the midsummer classic the most times in franchise history with eight. "Rapid Robert" appeared on the American League squad from 1938 to 1941, 1946 to 1948, and 1950. Feller was the starter for the AL in both 1941 and 1946. In the five games that Feller appeared, he was 1–0 with a 0.73 ERA and one save. He struck out 13.

Lou Boudreau, Larry Doby, Ken Keltner, and Bob Lemon all tied for second place with seven American League All-Star Game selections.

14. Cleveland defeated the Seattle Mariners by a score of 15–14 in 11 innings, and Cleveland tied the mark for overcoming the biggest run deficit in MLB history.

Both teams were in postseason contention, although under different circumstances, as they got ready for the Sunday evening, nationally televised game. Seattle stood at 80–30 record and held a healthy 20-game lead over Oakland in the American League West. Cleveland was 61–48 to this point in the season and was in second place in the Central. They trailed Minnesota by 1 1/2 games.

Seattle scored four runs in the second inning off Cleveland starter Dave Burba. Doubles by Al Martin, Tom Lampkin, and Mike Cameron and a two-out single by Ichiro Suzuki did the damage.

The Mariners started the third inning with six straight hits, a hit-by-pitch, a sacrifice fly, an error by shortstop Omar Vizquel, and another single to score eight runs in the frame. Burba was knocked out after giving up seven runs. Mike Bacsik relieved during the onslaught, making his major-league debut.

Cleveland scored two runs in the bottom of the fourth on Jim Thome's two-run homer. The Mariners lead was temporarily sliced to 10 runs until the top of the fifth when the M's scored two more times to reestablish their 12-run lead.

The score stood at 14–2 through six innings and perhaps Cleveland manager Charlie Manuel was starting to wave the white flag. He inserted substitutes for starters Juan González, Ellis Burks, Travis Fryman, and Roberto Alomar. Many of the 42,494 fans took note as many started to exit Jacobs Field.

Seattle starter Aaron Sele exited after 6 ⅔ innings, seemingly with an easy win in his back pocket. John Halama relieved him as Cleveland scored three more in the bottom of the seventh. Russell Branyan hit a solo shot off Sele and Jolbert Cabrera plated two with a bases-loaded single against Halama.

Cleveland inched closer with four runs in the bottom of eighth inning. Three of those runs came the way of the long ball. Thome hit his second homer, a solo shot to lead off the frame. Marty Cordova followed with a two-run shot.

The Mariners were still up, 14–9, as the bottom of the ninth inning began. Einar Díaz drove home two runs with a two-out bases-loaded single to left field. The Indians reloaded the bases, and Vizquel, down to his last strike, stroked a line drive past first base and into the right-field corner. The bases-loaded triple tied the score at 14 apiece.

Cleveland won it in the 11th inning when Kenny Lofton scored from second base on a broken-bat single by Cabrera. John Rocker, who came into the ballgame in the top of the inning, got the win as he struck out the side.

Seattle went on to win 116 games, breaking the AL record for most wins in a season that was held by the 1954 Cleveland Indians. Cleveland and Seattle met in the 2001 ALDS, with Seattle winning the series in five games.

15. Carlos Santana broke the 1–1 deadlock with his 17th home run in the top of the 19th inning. It was the longest game for the Indians since they went 22 innings at Minnesota on August 31, 1993. The victory set a new team record for consecutive games won, besting the 1942 and 1951 Indians teams who both had winning streaks of 13 games. Cleveland held a half-game lead over Kansas City when the streak began on June 17. When the streak ended on July 2, Cleveland held a six-game lead. The new record stood for just one season as the Tribe won 22 consecutive games from August 24 to September 14, 2017, setting a new AL record in the process.

It was a day for the pitchers. Cleveland's Josh Tomlin surrendered one earned run, as did the Blue Jays' Marcus Stroman. Both bullpens pitched scoreless ball until Santana's blast. Trevor Bauer, who was to start the next day, pitched five innings of scoreless relief for the win. Toronto manager John Gibbons ran out of pitchers and summoned infielders Ryan Goins and Darwin Barney into service. Goins pitched a scoreless frame while Barney took the loss. "What Trevor did was above and beyond," said Terry Francona. "We're pretty fortunate that he can do it and that he's willing to do it. Because one slip-up and we go home. You get so invested in a game like that. It shocked

Carlos Santana, who broke in as a catcher, moved to third base and eventually settled in at first, where he has developed into one of the better defensive players in baseball. In addition to his 174 home runs, Santana ranks fourth in franchise history in walks with 726. *AP Photo/Rick Scuteri.*

everybody. It feels good to win. It's the kind of game you wish you were playing at home because you're one bad pitch or slip-up [away] from going home with a loss after a long day."

Santana, who tied Mike Napoli for the team lead with 34 home runs in 2016, was 2-for-8 and scored both of the Indians' runs. Santana was an amateur free agent signed by the Los Angeles Dodgers on August 13, 2004. He was traded to Cleveland on July 26, 2008 with pitcher Jon Meloan for Casey Blake.

Santana was not the first Tribesman to accomplish this feat. On June 14, 1963, Willie Kirkland also homered to win a 19-inning game. Cleveland beat Washington, 3–2, at Cleveland Stadium in the nightcap of a doubleheader. Kirkland hit two home runs in the game. The first one by Willie knotted the score at two in the bottom of the 11th inning. Then he hit the game-winner in the 19th. On December 20, 2017, Santana signed a three-year, $60 million dollar contract with the Philadelphia Phillies.

16. Earl Averill (#3), Lou Boudreau (#5), Larry Doby (#14), Mel Harder (#18), Bob Feller (#19), Frank Robinson (#20), and Bob Lemon (#21) have all had their uniform numbers retired by the Cleveland Indians. With the exception of Harder, the rest of the players are all members of the National Baseball Hall of Fame in Cooperstown, New York.

Earl Averill (1929–39)—Played in 1,510 games with Cleveland. He batted .322, hit 226 home runs, 377 doubles, and had 1,903 hits. He also collected 1,084 RBIs. He was a six-time All-Star selection. Averill was elected to the Hall of Fame in 1975, and his number was retired the same year.

Lou Boudreau (1938–50)—Played in 1,560 games with Cleveland. He batted .296, scored 823 runs, hit 63 home runs and drove in 740 runs. Three times he led the American League in doubles and totaled 367. Boudreau was a seven-time All-Star selection. Boudreau also managed the Indians from 1942 to 1950. He compiled a 728–649 record for a .529 winning percentage. He ranks first among all managers in franchise history in wins. Boudreau was elected to the Hall of Fame in 1970, and his number was retired the same year.

Larry Doby (1947–55, 1958)—Played in 1,235 games for Cleveland. He batted .286, hit 215 home runs, 190 doubles, and collected 776 RBIs. He led the American League in home runs twice and RBIs once. Doby was the first African American player in the American League, making his debut on July 5, 1947. He was a seven-time All-Star selection. His number was retired in 1994. He was elected to the Hall of Fame in 1998.

Mel Harder (1928–47)—Pitched in 582 games for Cleveland. His record was 223–186 with a 3.80 ERA. Harder had two seasons of 20 or more wins and pitched 25 shutouts. Harder compiled 1,161 strikeouts and issued 1,118 walks. He was a four-time All-Star selection. After his pitching days were over, Harder served as a pitching coach for Cleveland, the New York Mets, Chicago Cubs, Cincinnati Reds, and Kansas City Royals between 1947 and 1969. His number was retired in 1990.

Bob Feller (1936–41, 1945–56)—Pitched in 570 games for Cleveland. His record was 266–162 with a 3.25 ERA. Feller had six seasons of 20 or more wins and threw 44 shutouts. He led the American League in wins six times, strikeouts seven times, and in innings pitched five times. Feller threw three no-hitters and 12 one-hitters. He was an eight-time All-Star selection. His number was retired in 1957. He was elected to the Hall of Fame in 1962.

Frank Robinson (1975–77)—Selected as the first African American manager in the major leagues in 1974. He made his managerial debut on April 8, 1975. He served as the designated hitter in the same game and hit a solo home run. "It was a tremendous day for me, a day I'll always remember, the

Frank Robinson is the only player in major-league history to be named MVP in each league: Cincinnati (1961) and Baltimore (1966). He has also been selected as Rookie of the Year (1956), Gold Glove winner (1958), Manager of the Year (1989), World Series MVP (1966), and All-Star Game MVP (1971).
Courtesy of Cleveland Public Library/Photograph Collection.

biggest day of my life in baseball," said Robinson. He compiled a 186–189 record for a winning percentage of .496. In 1981, he became manager of the San Francisco Giants, making him the first African American manager in the National League as well. His number was retired in 2017. Robinson was elected to the Hall of Fame in 1982.

Bob Lemon (1941–42, 1946–58)—Pitched in 460 games for Cleveland. His record was 207–128 with a 3.23 ERA. He threw 31 shutouts and totaled 1,277 strikeouts and issued 1,251 walks. Lemon had seven seasons of 20 or more wins. He led the league in wins three times, complete games five times, and innings pitched four times. He pitched a no-hitter against the Tigers in 1948. Lemon was a seven-time All-Star selection. His number was retired in 1998, and he was elected to Hall of Fame in 1976.

17. Jack Graney was the first batter to face Ruth, and he singled. He became the first former ballplayer to become a baseball radio broadcaster.

The native of St. Thomas, Ontario, came from a large family of nine children. Originally a pitcher, Graney was drafted by the Naps from Wilkes-Barre of the New York State League in 1907. Graney could really hum the old fastball, but he lacked control. After spending time in Portland, he returned to Cleveland in 1910, and he was turned into a left fielder. He was not known for his hitting, but he did get on base by way of the free pass.

Graney played all 14 years of his major-league career in Cleveland. For the Indians' 1920 world championship team, Graney was a platoon player but still hit .296 for the season. For his career, he hit .250 and walked 712 times, leading the league twice (1917, 1919).

After retiring as a player, Graney served as a broadcaster for the Indians on WHK radio. He served in this capacity from 1932 to 1953, with the exception of 1945. Graney was known as a master at recreating road games for the listeners back home, as he was familiar with all the nuances of the parks in the American League.

18. Cleveland manager Joe Gordon was swapped for Detroit skipper Jimmy Dykes. At the time of the trade, Cleveland was in fourth place and seven games out of first place in the American League standings. Detroit was in sixth place, 12 ½ games off the pace. The switch did not improve the performance of either team, as they remained in fourth and sixth place respectively at season's end.

The unprecedented move by Lane and DeWitt amused and bewildered others. Lane, who was vilified in Cleveland after trading Rocky Colavito to Detroit for Harvey Kuenn just four months earlier, was being laughed at again by the Cleveland fans.

Gordon was one of the best second baseman to ever play on the major-league level. He was a member of six pennant winners, five with the New York Yankees and one with Cleveland. He was the AL MVP in 1942 and was a nine-time All-Star selection.

Cleveland traded pitcher Allie Reynolds for Gordon on October 11, 1946. Gordon gave the Indians instant credibility because of his success with the Yankees. Although Reynolds went on to have a very successful career with New York, Gordon was an anchor of the Indians' world championship team in 1948. In four years with Cleveland, Gordon batted .262 with 100 home runs and 358 RBIs. Gordon, who had gymnastics training as a youngster, would often make what were described as "acrobatic" plays from his second base position. Together with Lou Boudreau at shortstop, the pair formed one of the most feared double-play combinations in baseball history.

Gordon was hired by Indians general manager Frank Lane in 1958 to replace Bobby Bragan as the Indians' manager. In 1959, he guided the Indians to a second-place finish.

Gordon passed away on April 14, 1978 as the result of a second heart attack. He was elected to the Hall of Fame in 2009.

Jimmy Dykes was a baseball lifer. He had a 22-year career as a player (1918–39) with the Philadelphia Athletics and the Chicago White Sox. He managed for 21 seasons, compiling a record of 1,406–1,541 for a winning percentage of .477. He served another ten years as a coach on the major league level. Primarily a middle infielder in his playing days, Dykes was a solid, dependable player. In 2,282 games, he batted .280 with 108 home runs and 1,069 RBIs.

Dykes passed away on June 15, 1976 from an undisclosed illness.

19. Larry Doby, who was the first African American ballplayer in the American League, became the first to hit a home run in a World Series Game.

On October 9, 1948, Doby smashed a solo home run to right-center field off of the Boston Brave's Johnny Sain. "It was a change of pace," said Doby when asked what kind of pitch he hit his home run on. "Although even Sain's change of pace is quicker than most pitchers' fast ones. I sort of hitched on the pitch when he let up on me, but I got a real full swing and hit it with power, even though maybe it didn't look that way from upstairs."

Doby's shot gave Cleveland a 2–0 lead, and they hung on to win, 2–1, in Game Four of the World Series at Cleveland Stadium. The win gave Cleveland a commanding 3–1 series lead. Sain proceeded to retire the next 16 of 17 batters he faced, but the Braves could only muster one run off of Cleveland starter Steve Gromek. The right-hander scattered seven hits, striking out two in nine innings of work.

The following day, a picture of Gromek and Doby embracing after the Indians' win was on the front page of many newspapers across the country. It became an iconic photo of two men, one white, one black, sharing a glorious moment. With the integration of major league baseball just one year old and all the emotions that came out because of it, the photo spoke volumes. For many, it was just not something they had ever seen before.

20. Danny Ainge, who was the starting third baseman for the Blue Jays, went 0-for-2 on the evening. He grounded out to second base in the third inning and struck out in the sixth. Ainge was lifted in the top of the ninth inning for pinch-hitter Al Woods.

Ainge was drafted by Toronto out of BYU in the 15th round in 1977. Ainge was assigned to Triple-A Syracuse of the International League in 1978. Over the next two seasons, Ainge split his seasons between Toronto and Syracuse. He did not hit above .250 in any season, minor- or major-league ball. He left baseball after three seasons and 211 major league games with a lifetime batting average of .220.

Ainge was also a basketball star at BYU, as he averaged 24.4 points per game his senior year. He was a second-round draft pick of the Boston Celtics in 1981 NBA draft. Ainge went on to have a 14-year career in the NBA and was part of two world championship teams with Boston in 1984 and 1986. In 1,042 games, he averaged 11.5 points per game and shot 84.6 percent from the free throw line and 37.8 percent from three-point land.

As of 2018, Ainge is the general manager/president of basketball operations for the Boston Celtics.

21. Albert Belle led the American League with 50 home runs and tied Seattle's Edgar Martínez for the league lead with 52 doubles in 1995.

Belle and Martínez were also tied with the most runs with 121, and Belle had the league's top slugging percentage at .690. Belle and Boston's Mo Vaughn tied with the league lead in RBIs with 126.

Belle, of Shreveport, Louisiana, was the Indians' second-round pick out of LSU in the 1987 amateur draft. After Belle spent two seasons in Class A ball, he took the Eastern League by storm. He belted 20 home runs, drove in 69 runs, and batted .282 in 89 games for Canton-Akron in 1989.

Belle earned a promotion to the Indians, making his major-league debut against Texas on July 15, 1989. In his first at-bat, Belle singled to left field and drove in a run against Nolan Ryan.

Belle spent most of the 1990 season at Triple-A Colorado Springs but returned to the Indians in 1991. He was one of the few bright spots in a season that saw Cleveland lose 105 games. Belle smacked 28 home runs, drove in 95 runs, and batted .282.

Belle was one of the top power hitters in the major leagues, as well as one of its top run producers. In each of the next nine seasons he topped 100 RBIs, leading the AL three times. He also topped 30 or more home runs in the next eight seasons.

In eight seasons with Cleveland, Belle played 913 games. He totaled 242 home runs, 223 doubles, and 751 RBIs. His batting average while wearing an Indians uniform was .295. He ranks second in franchise history with a .580 slugging percentage.

While with Baltimore in 2001, Belle was forced to retire because of a degenerative hip condition.

22. As of 2017, the Cleveland Indians have never had a pitcher win a Gold Glove Award. Below is the list of winners by position.

Catcher	– Ray Fosse (1970–71), Sandy Alomar Jr. (1990)
First Base	– Vic Power (1958–61)
Second Base	– Roberto Alomar (1999–2001)
Shortstop	– Omar Vizquel (1994–2001), Francisco Lindor (2016)
Third Base	– Matt Williams (1997), Travis Fryman (2000)
Outfield	– Minnie Miñoso (1959), Jim Piersall (1961), Vic Davalillo (1964), Rick Manning (1976), Kenny Lofton (1993–96), Grady Sizemore (2007–08)

23. Jason Kipnis hit at least one home run in each round of the postseason. He hit one each in the Division Series and the League Championship Series and connected for two home runs in the World Series.

Kipnis was originally drafted in the fourth round by the San Diego Padres out of Arizona State University in 2008 but did not sign. The next year he was drafted by Cleveland in the second round and signed with them.

Kipnis was an outfielder in college and in his early pro career. He was shifted to second base in 2010 when he got to Class A Kinston and then Double-A Akron in 2010. His star shone brightly at Triple-A Columbus in 2011 where he batted .280 with

12 home runs and 55 RBIs in 92 games. He earned a call up to Cleveland and made his major-league debut on July 22, 2011.

He became the starting second baseman for the Indians in 2012 and has been selected to two All-Star Games.

24. Joe Sewell, a twenty-one-year-old rookie, was signed from the New Orleans Pelicans to replace Harry Lunte, who had pulled a muscle in his leg. Lunte had been pressed into the vacated shortstop position, but once he was injured, he was unable to continue and in stepped Sewell.

Sewell was born October 9, 1898, in Titus, Alabama. His younger brothers, Luke and Tommy, also played in the major leagues.

After high school, Joe enrolled at the University of Alabama. Although small in stature, 5-foot-5 and 155 pounds, Joe played like a giant on both the gridiron and the baseball diamond. Upon his graduation from college, Joe bypassed the wishes of his parents to enroll at medical school and signed his first professional baseball contract with the Class A New Orleans Pelicans of the Southern Association. One of his many attributes was the ability to get his bat on the ball. He made contact with ease. "When I was a boy, I'd walk around with a pocket full of rocks or a Coca-Cola top, and I can't remember not being able to hit them with a broomstick handle."

Sewell did not only make contact, but he batted a respectable .289 for the Pelicans. But once Lunte pulled up lame, Sewell was on a train northward. He made his debut on September 10, and the rest, as they say, is history.

Sewell played in the remaining 22 games of the season, batting .329. Because Cleveland signed him so late in the season, Sewell would not have been eligible for the World Series.

But Brooklyn manager Wilbert Robinson agreed to let Sewell participate due to the circumstances.

He did not fare so well in the fall classic, batting .174. But despite the rookie's lack of production, the Indians claimed the first world championship in franchise history.

Over the next 10 seasons, Sewell was a force offensively. In his 11 years with Cleveland, Sewell batted .320 with 30 home runs, 375 doubles, and 868 RBIs. But perhaps the most amazing statistic is that in 5,621 at bats, Sewell only struck out 99 times. In 1925, Sewell had 608 at–bats and struck out four times. In 1929, Sewell had 578 at-bats and again only struck out four times. At one point that season, Sewell went 115 straight games without being rung up (May 19 to September 19).

In the last two years in Cleveland, Sewell was moved to third base. He was released on January 20, 1931. The New York Yankees signed him four days later, and he was their starting third baseman for three years. Sewell was a part of another world championship team in 1932 when the Yankees swept the Chicago Cubs.

The University of Alabama has named their baseball stadium Sewell-Thomas Stadium in honor of former Tide baseball coach Frank Thomas and Joe Sewell. Many simply refer to the stadium as "The Joe."

Sewell passed away on March 6, 1990.

25. Adrian "Addie" Joss was the Cleveland pitcher who passed away as a result of tubercular meningitis on April 14, 1911. Joss pitched for Cleveland from 1902 to 1910. He compiled a record of 160–97 with 1.89 ERA. He totaled 920 strikeouts against 364 walks. He had four seasons of 20 or more wins. In 1907, he led the American League in wins.

The Naps were headed northward to begin the 1911 season when they stopped in Chattanooga, Tennessee, on April 3 for an exhibition game. Joss, who had been having arm problems, was talking to a friend when he fainted. His condition worsened as he headed home to Toledo to confer with his physician. He was diagnosed with an attack of pleurisy. Two days after his thirty-first birthday, Joss passed away.

His funeral was held on April 17. The Naps were playing a series against the Tigers and attended the funeral, along with some members of the Detroit team. The Naps decided to hold a benefit game for Joss's wife, Lillian, and their two children.

The date was set for July 24, 1911, at League Park. A team of All-Stars would take on the Naps. It was an incredible ensemble of baseball royalty that showed up in Cleveland that day.

The All-Stars were led by Walter Johnson, Tris Speaker, Ty Cobb, Eddie Collins, Sam Crawford, Home Run Baker, Smoky Joe Wood, Hal Chase, and Clyde Milan. The Naps were led by Shoeless Joe Jackson, Napoleon Lajoie, Cy Young, George Stovall, Terry Turner, Ivy Olson, and Joe Birmingham. The gate was announced at 15,270. The All-Stars won the game, 5–3. The receipts totaled $12,914.

2
STARTING LINEUP
LEVEL

STARTING LINEUP LEVEL

(Answers begin on page 51)

1. Who is the only pitcher in Cleveland Indians history to win at least 30 games in a season?

2. Bob Feller is the only pitcher in major-league history to pitch a no-hitter on opening day. What was the year, the opposing team, and at which stadium did "Rapid Robert" accomplish this feat?

3. In 1987, the Indians had two pitchers on their staff who were later enshrined into the Hall of Fame. Who were they?

4. The Indians have had two players who each enjoyed a 30-30 season (30 home runs and 30 stolen bases). Who were they?

5. In Game Three of the 1997 American League Championship Series at Jacobs Field, how was the winning run scored to give Cleveland a 2–1 victory over Baltimore?

6. On July 19, 1974, Dick Bosman pitched a no-hitter against the Oakland Athletics. On May 30, 1977, Dennis Eckersley pitched a no-hitter against the California Angels. Name the player who was in the starting lineup at the same position for both games.

7. On May 30, 1977, Dennis Eckersley pitched a no-hitter against the California Angels. On May 15, 1981, Len Barker pitched a perfect game against the Toronto Blue

Jays. Name the two players who were in the starting lineup at the same positions for both games.

8. Who pitched the first no-hitter in Cleveland Stadium history?

9. As of 2017, who was the last Cleveland Indian to hit for the cycle?

10. On April 6, 1992, this Cleveland Indian was credited with the first hit at Baltimore's Oriole Park at Camden Yards. Two nights later, this same player hit the first home run there. Who is he?

11. In 2005, which Indians pitcher led the American League with a 2.86 ERA, but posted a losing record of 9–11?

12. Who are the only two pitchers to exceed 2,000 strikeouts while wearing a Cleveland uniform?

13. In 1965, Rocky Colavito led the American League in RBIs with 108. In 1986, Joe Carter led the AL in RBIs with 121. In the 21 years between the two Indian RBI champs, only one other Indians player drove in more than 100 runs in a season. Who was he?

14. Who was the first pitcher to win a World Series Game at Cleveland Stadium?

15. There are three players in the 3,000 hit club who reached that plateau while they wore a Cleveland uniform. Who were they?

16. On August 21, 1920, Cleveland acquired a left-handed pitcher from Sacramento of the Pacific Coast League. The southpaw proved to be quite an addition to the pitching staff as he posted a 7–0 record with a 1.85 ERA in just over a month's work. His efforts helped the

Indians win their first pennant that year. Then the lefty shut out Brooklyn in Game Six of the World Series. Who was he?

17. The first game at Jacobs Field (now Progressive Field) was played on April 4, 1994 when Cleveland beat Seattle, 4–3. Which Indians player singled in the winning run in the 11th inning?

18. On July 14, 2002, this Indians player capped a six-run ninth inning with a grand slam off Mariano Rivera. The home run to right field gave Cleveland a 10–7 victory over New York. Who was this Tribe player?

19. Who has appeared in the most games while wearing a Cleveland uniform?

20. Which Indians pitcher was credited with a save in the 1989 All-Star Game at Anaheim?

21. Cleveland acquired first baseman Mike Hargrove from San Diego on June 14, 1979. Who did the Indians send to the Padres in exchange?

22. This Indians pitcher posted a 2–0 record in the 1948 World Series. However, six years later, he went 0–2 in the fall classic. Who was this Indians pitcher?

23. Since the inception of interleague play in 1997, four Cleveland pitchers have hit a home run. One of them did it twice. Who was he?

24. Which Indians catcher holds the club record for most home runs in a single season?

25. Who was the last Cleveland Indian to be voted American League Most Valuable Player Award by the Baseball Writers Association of America?

STARTING LINEUP LEVEL — ANSWERS

1. Jim Bagby Sr. posted a 31–12 record in 1920. Ironically, Bagby turned thirty-one later that year during the World Series. He led the league in wins, complete games (30), and innings pitched (339 2/3). Stan Coveleski added 24 wins, and Ray Caldwell chipped in with 20 as Cleveland won its first American League pennant. But Bagby was the workhorse of the staff. He won his first eight decisions of the season and was 14–3 at the end of June. On July 19, Bagby pitched in both ends of a doubleheader at Boston. In the opener, Bagby got the win after pitching 2 2/3 innings of relief as Cleveland was victorious, 10–6. He started and got a no-decision in the nightcap. After eight innings, Bagby gave way to George Uhle, who took the loss as the Red Sox won, 5–4, in ten innings.

The pennant race in 1920 was a three-way fight between the Indians, the Chicago White Sox, and New York. Bagby went 5–2 in September and 1–1 in October. Ultimately, Chicago was left short-handed when indictments were handed down for seven of their players who were accused of throwing the 1919 World Series. With three games remaining on the White Sox schedule, the accused players were suspended. (Chick Gandil had retired from baseball after the 1919 season. However, he was still held accountable for his part in the fix.) The Yankees faded, and Cleveland won the pennant.

Bagby went 1–1 in the World Series, both times matching up against Brooklyn's Burleigh Grimes. Cleveland won their

Jim Bagby pitched seven seasons with the Tribe and recorded double-digits wins in all but one. He is one of only thirteen pitchers in the big leagues to win 30 or more games in a season since 1900. *Courtesy of Cleveland Public Library/Photograph Collection.*

first world championship over the Brooklyn Robins in seven games (the World Series was a nine game series that year).

Bagby retired after the 1923 season. In seven seasons with Cleveland, he posted a record of 122–86 with a 3.03 ERA.

2. Bob Feller threw his first no-hitter on April 16, 1940 against the Chicago White Sox at Comiskey Park. It was a cold, raw day in the Windy City as the Indians topped the Chisox, 1–0. There have been many other games where Feller was sharper then he was on this day. He walked five batters and struck out eight.

Like many no-hitters that are thrown, Feller was the recipient of some fine defensive plays behind him. "I had some pretty fancy support out there," said Feller. "Ben Chapman saved my bacon twice and Kenny [Keltner] and Ray [Mack] each made a couple of swell plays. Sure, I had pretty good stuff, but I was lucky too." Feller singled out Mack, saying "Mack came up with two as sweet plays as I've ever seen. He was way off balance when he scooped up [Larry] Rosenthal's roller in the eighth, and how his throw ever beat Larry to the bag I don't know. And I don't know how he ever knocked down [Taffy] Wright's smash in the ninth, to say nothing of retrieving the ball and throwing the guy out."

Cleveland scored their lone run in the top of the fourth inning. With one down, Jeff Heath singled to left field. After a fly out, Rollie Hemsley tripled to score Heath.

Feller threw two more no-hitters in his career. The second one occurred on April 30, 1946 against New York at Yankee Stadium. The Indians won again by the score of 1–0 as Frankie Hayes hit a solo home run in the top of the ninth inning. Feller struck out 11 and walked five Yankee hitters.

Bob Feller is the face of the Cleveland Indians franchise. In spite of his many successes on the pitcher's mound, Feller is also remembered as enlisting in the United States Navy two days after the attack on Pearl Harbor. He served as member of the gunnery crew on the battleship *USS Alabama* in World War II.
Courtesy of Cleveland Public Libary/Photograph Collection.

His third and final no-hit game came on July 1, 1951 at Cleveland Stadium. Cleveland topped Detroit, 2–1. The Tigers scored their run on two errors, one by Feller and one by shortstop Ray Boone, a stolen base and a sacrifice fly. Luke Easter drove in both runs for the Tribe. Feller struck out five and walked three batters.

Perhaps the most impressive statistic about Feller is the 12 one-hitters that he pitched in his career. That mark is a major-league record.

Although there have been pitchers who have thrown no-hitters on days that appeared on the calendar before April 16, Feller's effort was still the only one on opening day.

3. Phil Niekro and Steve Carlton were the two future Hall of Fame pitchers who were on the Cleveland Indians in 1987. On April 9, 1987, the pair made history as they became the first two 300-game winners in major-league history to appear in the same game as teammates. In a 14–3 Indians victory at Toronto, Niekro started the game and got the win. Carlton pitched the final four innings and was credited with a save.

Phil Niekro had joined the club in 1986 and instantly became a fan favorite. His command of the knuckleball and his forty-seven years of age endeared many to "Knucksie." His record in 1986 was 11–11 with a 4.32 ERA. Niekro also served as a mentor for Tom Candiotti, who also threw the knuckleball.

Cleveland finished 84–78 in 1986 and enthusiasm was high for the 1987 season. But the Tribe played poorly and they were on their way to a 100-loss season. They traded Niekro (7–11, 5.89) to Toronto for two prospects on August 9. In a career that spanned 24 years, Niekro hurled primarily for the Atlanta Braves. He won 20 games or more in three different seasons. In 1979, Niekro led the National League in both wins (21) and losses (20). One of Niekro's most interesting seasons was in 1977. His record was 16–20, yet he led the league in strikeouts with 262.

Niekro was 318–274 for his career, with a 3.35 ERA. He totaled 245 complete games, 45 shutouts, and 3,342 strikeouts. He was elected to the Hall of Fame in 1997.

Steve Carlton, like Niekro, played most of his career in the National League. He also had a 24-year career. Carlton signed with Cleveland as a free agent on April 4, 1987. His record was 5–9 with a 5.37 ERA before the Indians traded him to Minnesota on July 31.

Carlton, a southpaw who was known simply as "Lefty," was a much different pitcher then Niekro. Where Niekro used a knuckleball as his primary pitch, Carlton was all speed and a terrific slider. He racked up four Cy Young Awards (1972, 1977, 1980, and 1982). For his career, Carlton was 329–244 with an ERA of 3.22. He totaled 4,136 strikeouts, 254 complete games, and 55 shutouts. He exceeded the 200-strikeout mark in eight seasons. Lefty won 20 or more games six times.

Perhaps his most impressive season was in 1972 with Philadelphia when he went 27–10, with a 1.97 ERA and 310 strikeouts. The Phillies' record that year was 59–97. Carlton won 45.7 percent of their victories.

He was a member of four pennant-winning teams, and two world champion clubs (St. Louis, 1967, and Philadelphia, 1980). Carlton was elected to the Hall of Fame in 1994 on the first ballot, garnering 95.6 percent of the vote.

4. Joe Carter in 1987 (32 home runs and 31 stolen bases) and Grady Sizemore in 2008 (33 home runs, 38 stolen bases) are the only two players in franchise history to accomplish this feat.

Joe Carter had every intention of being a two-sport star when he enrolled at Wichita State. Even though he was ticketed to be the Shockers' starting quarterback, he gravitated to baseball. Validation of his decision came when *The Sporting News* named him their College Player of the Year in 1981. That season Carter set a then-collegiate record of 120 RBIs and batted .411 with 24 home runs.

He was selected with the second overall pick by the Chicago Cubs in the June 1981 amateur draft. Carter spent the next three years in the Chicago farm system before he was traded to Cleveland on June 13, 1984. Carter was packaged with outfielder Mel Hall, pitcher Don Schulze, and prospect Daryl Banks for pitcher Rick Sutcliffe and catcher Ron Hassey.

Carter was a solid player on teams that were not very competitive. In 1985 and 1987, the Indians had more than 100 losses. In 1986, Carter led the American League in RBIs with 121 and set career highs in batting average (.302) and hits (200). It was the only season while Carter wore a Cleveland uniform that the Indians finished over .500 and they had their best finish in the AL East, fifth place.

With one year remaining on his contract after the 1989 season, it was a sure bet that Carter would not be signing with the Indians as a free agent. Cleveland traded him to San Diego on December 6, 1989, for Sandy Alomar Jr., Carlos Baerga, and Chris James.

Carter signed a three-year deal with San Diego, but was then involved in a blockbuster deal yet again. Carter and second baseman Roberto Alomar were traded to Toronto for first baseman Fred McGriff and shortstop Tony Fernández on December 5, 1990.

The Toronto Blue Jays won three straight AL East titles from 1991 to 1993 and two world championships in 1992 and 1993. Carter was a big reason as he was finally recognized for his ability. Carter was selected to participate in the All-Star Game for the first of four consecutive years in 1991.

Carter personally delivered a world title to Toronto when he homered off the Phillies' Mitch Williams in Game Six of the 1993 World Series. The three-run blast in the bottom of the ninth inning gave the Blue Jays an 8–6 win. It was the second time in major-league history that a World Series ended with a home run.

Carter's last season in the big leagues was in 1998 with Baltimore and San Francisco. In six years with Cleveland, Carter batted .269 with 151 home runs, 530 RBIs, and 126 stolen bases in 839 games.

Like Carter, **Grady Sizemore** starred in football and baseball and signed a scholarship to play both sports at the University of Washington. But when the Montreal Expos picked Sizemore in the third round of the amateur draft in 2000, Sizemore opted for professional baseball.

He was not with the Expos organization long. On June 27, 2002, Sizemore was packaged with first baseman Lee Stevens, second baseman Brandon Phillips, and pitcher Cliff Lee in a deal that sent them to Cleveland for pitchers Bartolo Colón and Tim Drew.

In 2003, Sizemore hit .304 at Double-A Akron with 13 home runs and 78 RBIs in 128 games. He was promoted to Triple-A Buffalo in 2004. Hit offensive ability continued to blossom, batting .287 and driving in 51 runs in 101 games for the Bisons.

He was called up to Cleveland, making his major-league debut on July 21, 2004. From 2005 to 2008, Sizemore was the symbol of both stability and production from his center-field position. From 2006 to 2008 he led the league in games started, and he hit for power and average. He was elected to the All-Star Game three years in a row (2006–08) and won the Gold Glove Award in 2007 and 2008.

Sizemore's 2009 season was cut short when he had surgery on his left elbow. In 2010, he injured his left knee and appeared in just 33 games. Microfracture surgery was required, thus ending his season. He returned to Cleveland in 2011, but a right knee contusion and a sports hernia injury limited him to 71 games.

Sizemore was sidelined for the 2012 and 2013 seasons due to an injured back and microfracture surgery on his right knee.

He attempted comebacks with Boston, Philadelphia, and Tampa Bay but he could not regain his past ability. In 892 games with Cleveland, Sizemore batted .269 with 139 home runs, 458 RBIs, and 134 stolen bases.

In 2017, Sizemore joined the Indians' front office as a player development advisor.

5. Marquis Grissom went from goat to hero with his steal of home plate in the 12th inning to deliver a 2–1 victory.

For those baseball fans that enjoy low scoring pitching duels, Game Three of the 1997 ALCS was for them. Baltimore started Mike Mussina while Cleveland tapped Orel Hershiser to toe the slab. Both pitchers were on the top of their game, as through six innings there was no score.

Cleveland scored first in the bottom of the seventh inning when Jim Thome walked, David Justice singled to center field, and Matt Williams followed suit and Thome scored.

Mussina was spectacular. He struck out 15 batters in seven innings. At one point, he struck out five Indians in a row. Mussina gave way to the bullpen after seven innings.

Hershiser also exited after seven innings. Jose Mesa entered the game in the top of the ninth inning to try and shut down the Orioles and preserve the 1–0 win. But Chris Hoiles singled to start the inning and was lifted for pinch-runner Jeff Reboulet. Jeffrey Hammonds pinch-hit for Mike Bordick and grounded out, as Reboulet moved up to second base. Brady Anderson stepped to the plate and lifted a high fly ball to center field. Marquis Grissom lost the ball in the lights, and it landed behind him as Reboulet raced home with the tying run.

Each team's bullpens were as stingy as the starters. Zeros again populated the scoreboard. In the bottom of the 12th inning, left-hander Randy Myers was pitching for the Orioles. With one out, he walked Grissom. Tony Fernández singled to right field and Grissom sped to third base. Omar Vizquel was the next batter, and being a switch-hitter, batted from the right side of the plate.

Cleveland manager Mike Hargrove called for a squeeze play. "I started thinking squeeze right away. There are certain players you can do certain things with."

With the count 2-1, Grissom took off from third base. Vizquel offered at the pitch, but he missed it and the baseball glanced off the mitt of Orioles catcher Lenny Webster. The ball rolled away, but Webster did not give pursuit. "He definitely tipped the ball and deflected it off my glove," said Webster.

"I saw contact. I heard contact. When [umpire John] Hirschbeck gestured, I thought he meant it was a foul ball. That's why I didn't run after it."

Grissom crossed the plate and was given credit for a stolen base. The win gave Cleveland a 2–1 series lead. They would eventually defeat the Orioles in six games, winning their second pennant in three years.

6. Buddy Bell was the starting third baseman for both no-hit games. In the first game on July 19, 1974, Bell went 2-for-3 with a double, a run, and an RBI. He had no putouts and five assists. In the second game on May 30, 1977, Bell went 0-for-2 with a walk. He had no putouts and no assists.

Frank Duffy started at shortstop for Bosman's no-hitter. In Eckersley's, he was a defensive replacement for Larvell Blanks in the top of the eighth inning.

Buddy Bell is the son of former Cincinnati Reds and Pittsburgh Pirates outfielder Gus Bell. He attended Archbishop Moeller High School in Cincinnati and was Cleveland's 16th round pick in the June 1969 amateur draft.

Bell came into his own at Triple-A Wichita of the American Association in 1971. In 129 games, he led the Aeros in hits (136) and runs (65). Bell was second in home runs (11), RBIs (59), doubles (23), and hit .289. He played 113 games at third base where he fielded his position at a .954 clip.

However, Cleveland had Graig Nettles at third base. Bell was promoted to the Indians for the 1972 season but was moved to the outfield. He split his time between center and right field. Cleveland dealt Nettles to the New York Yankees after the season and Bell was inserted as the starting third baseman for the next six seasons.

Bell was a consummate pro. He was steady in the field and at the plate. He was a fan favorite, easily one of the most popular players during his time in Cleveland. You won't find his name among the franchise leaders in any offensive category, but he will always remain one of the few bright spots of those Indians teams in the 1970s.

He also had a lot of class. In 1975, Bell was chosen by Oakland manager Al Dark as Cleveland's representative for the All-Star Game. Bell declined, citing his batting average and insisting that there were other players more deserving.

"I wanted Buddy because I think he could help us win the game," said Dark. "There's no doubt but that Buddy is one of the stars of baseball and belongs in the All-Star Game. I'd be honored to have him on the team. But I couldn't convince him.

"Once he made his decision, and I knew it was irrevocable, I told Buddy I admire his attitude and his courage for doing what he thinks is right, no matter the consequences. And now I have even more respect for Buddy Bell."

In the seven seasons Bell played for Cleveland, he batted .274 with 64 home runs and 386 RBIs. In a trade that truly upset the locals, Bell was dealt to Texas for Toby Harrah on December 8, 1978.

He flourished in Texas, winning the Gold Glove Award each season from 1979 to 1984. In that span his lowest batting average was .277. Bell was a four-time All-Star with Texas (1980, 1981, 1982, and 1984). He was traded to Cincinnati in 1985 and was a member of his hometown team until 1988 when he was dealt to Houston. He rejoined Texas in 1989 but retired during the season.

Bell retired from baseball with a batting average of .279, 201 home runs, 1,106 RBIs, and 2,514 hits in 2,405 games over 18 seasons. He ranks fourth all-time in games played without appearing in the postseason, behind Ernie Banks, Luke Appling, and Mickey Vernon.

Buddy's two sons, David and Mike, both played in the major leagues. With his father Gus, the Bells are one of four three-generation families in the majors, joining the Hairston, Boone, and Coleman families.

However, he did not stray too far from the game that he loved. In 1990 he joined the Cleveland organization as a roving minor-league hitting instructor. He moved on to Chicago, where he was the director of minor league instruction for the White Sox from 1991 through 1993. He then returned to the Indians for two seasons as their bench coach.

Bell managed at the major league level with Detroit (1996–98), Colorado (2000–02), and Kansas City (2005–07). He served on manager Eric Wedge's staff in Cleveland as the bench coach from 2003 through May 30, 2005. His managerial record was 519–724 for a .418 winning percentage.

He spent nine years working in the front office of the Chicago White Sox (2008–17). In 2016, he was named the recipient of the Sheldon "Chief" Bender Award given annually to an individual with distinguished service who has been instrumental in player development.

After the 2017 season, Bell left the White Sox to take a position with Cincinnati as a vice president and senior advisor to president of baseball operations/general manager Dick Williams.

7. Duane Kuiper started at second base for both games while Rick Manning was the starting center fielder.

Kuiper hit his second triple of the season in the first inning on May 30, 1977. He scored the only run of the game when Jim Norris laid down a sacrifice bunt as Kuiper scored. Manning was 0-for-3 at the plate with four putouts.

In Barker's perfect game, Manning singled to lead off the first inning and went to third on an error by Toronto first baseman John Mayberry. He scored on a sacrifice fly by Andre Thornton for the first Cleveland run. Manning made four putouts, including the last one to secure the perfect game, a fly ball off the bat of Toronto's Ernie Whitt.

Kuiper went 0-for-3 with five assists. Kuiper made terrific plays to his left and to his right to get two groundouts.

Both Kuiper and Manning had careers that in many ways paralleled each other. Both came up through the Indians' farm system at almost the same time, as they were teammates at both Class A Reno of the California League and Triple-A Oklahoma City of the American Association. Kuiper was a little ahead of Manning, making his major-league debut in 1974. But he was sent back down to the minors in 1975 when Jack Brohamer beat him out for the second base job.

Frank Robinson, Cleveland's new manager in 1975, wanted an infusion of youth into an otherwise lackluster team. Both Kuiper and Manning excelled, with speed and defense as their calling cards. Manning could cover the ground with the best of them and Kuiper could go to his right or left to make the play from second base.

Manning won a Gold Glove for defensive excellence in 1976. He had some "pop" in his bat and was destined for stardom until he injured his back on June 4, 1977 in the Seattle Kingdome. Manning injured his back sliding into second base. Being the athlete that he was, Manning kept playing but the pain kept getting worse. Eventually his back was put into a brace, and when he returned, a lot of his raw speed was gone.

He was not getting the infield hits like when he first came up. After hitting .292 in 1976, his production dropped. His defense was still superb, as he could still cover ground. But the same fans who would cheer his hustle, now booed to what they perceived as loafing.

Kuiper suffered a knee injury after a collision with Seattle's Tom Paciorek on June 1, 1980. He needed surgery on his right knee to repair cartilage and ligament damage. He was out until May of 1981. One of his first games back was Barker's perfect game, and he played brilliantly.

But Kuiper was traded in the offseason to San Francisco for pitcher Ed Whitson. Manning was dealt during the 1983 season to Milwaukee with pitcher Rick Waits for outfielder Gorman Thomas and pitchers Jamie Easterly and Ernie Camacho.

Kuiper retired after the 1985 season, while Manning retired after the 1987 campaign. Both individuals have moved to the broadcast booth, and they are two of the best commentators in the game.

In nine years with Cleveland and 1,063 games, Manning had a batting average of .263 with 36 home runs, 336 RBIs, and 142 stolen bases. For his career, he fielded .986 at his center field position.

In eight years with Cleveland and 786 games, Kuiper had a batting average of .274 with one home run and 221 RBIs. For his career, he fielded .983 at his second base position.

8. Don Black pitched the first no-hitter at Cleveland Stadium on July 10, 1947.

He defeated the Philadelphia Athletics by a score of 3–0. Black struck out five batters but also walked six. All three runs were scored in the bottom of the second inning. Consecutive singles by Eddie Robinson and Joe Gordon put runners on the corners. One out later, Jim Hegan hit a ball that struck the second-base bag and bounded into center field. Robinson scored as Gordon raced to third base. Black followed with a bunt down the first base line. The baseball hugged the line as Gordon raced home with the second run as Black was thrown out. George Metkovich singled home Hegan with the final tally. In addition to his sacrifice, Black recorded two hits in the game. The game only took 1:43 to play and a crowd of 47, 871 were in attendance.

Don Black, a native of Salix, Iowa, was signed by the Philadelphia Athletics in 1943 for $5,000 after he threw two no-hitters for Petersburg of the Virginia League. The first no-hitter was on July 22, 1941, a 1–0 win over the Staunton Presidents. Black's second no-hitter occurred a year later on August 4, 1942, a 4–0 victory over the Pulaski Counts.

Black's addiction to alcohol severely hampered his pitching ability. A's owner Connie Mack gave him multiple opportunities to straighten out, but Black would, or could not conform. Philadelphia outfielder Charlie Metro related a story about how Black staggered into the dining room at a Boston hotel and joined a table for breakfast. Black ordered a bowl of split pea soup. "We're eating our eggs and he's fumbling with the spoon to eat his soup, and [Al] Simmons moves over a little to block Mr. Mack's view of what's going on, and the guy leans over to spoon up soup and falls face down right into the bowl. We're all moving in close to cover it up and Connie Mack says 'You don't have to do that. I've seen it.'"

Black was suspended for thirty days without pay. He returned to finish out the season, but his days with the Athletics were all but over. Black was sold to Cleveland for $7,500 after the season.

Black pitched in Cleveland for the next three seasons, but he could not shake his addiction. On September 13, 1948, Black was at bat in the second inning in a game against St. Louis. He suffered a cerebral hemorrhage. While he did recover, he never played again in the major leagues.

For his career, Black was 34–55 with a 4.35 ERA. He passed away on April 21, 1959 after collapsing at his home while watching an Indians game. He was rushed to a hospital where he was pronounced dead. He was forty-two years old.

9. Rajai Davis hit for the cycle on July 2, 2016 at the Rogers Centre in Toronto.

Davis led off the first inning with his ninth home run. He tripled in the third, doubled in the seventh, and singled in the ninth inning. On the day Davis was 4-for-5 with two runs and two RBIs. He also stole a base. Cleveland lost to Toronto, 9–6, snapping their then-franchise-best 14-game winning streak.

Davis was originally selected by Pittsburgh in the 38th round of the free agent draft in 2001. He traveled quite a bit in his career, making stops in Pittsburgh (2006–07), San Francisco (2007–08), Oakland (2008–10), Toronto (2011–13), Detroit (2014–15), and Cleveland (2016). Davis rejoined the Athletics in 2017 and was dealt to Boston late in the season.

Davis led the American League in stolen bases with 43 in 2016, becoming the sixth different player in Cleveland history to do so. The others to do so were Harry Bay (1903–04), Elmer Flick (1904, 1906), George Case (1946), and Kenny Lofton (1992–96). Bay and Flick tied for the league lead in 1904 with 38 thefts.

Davis might best be remembered for his heroics in Game Seven of the 2016 World Series at Progessive Field, when he tied the score at six with a two-out, two-run home run in the eighth inning. The game went 10 innings before the Chicago Cubs eventually won, 8–7.

10. Paul Sorrento singled in the top of the second inning of the 1992 season opener for the first hit at Camden Yards. The Orioles won the game, 2–0. Sorrento connected for a three-run homer against Baltimore starting pitcher Bob Milacki in the first inning on April 8. Cleveland went on to win, 4–0, as Mark Lewis added a solo shot in the fifth inning.

Sorrento was drafted out of Florida State University by the California Angels in the fourth round in 1986. He was dealt as part of a five-player deal to Minnesota on November 3, 1988.

Sorrento was promoted from Double-A Orlando of the Southern League to make his major-league debut on September 8, 1989. Over the next two seasons, Sorrento split his seasons between the Twins and Triple-A Portland of the Pacific Coast League. He had little difficulty hitting at the Triple-A level. Sorrento hit 19 home runs and drove in 72 runs, while batting .302 for the Beavers in 1990. He came back in 1991 to hit 13 home runs with 79 RBIs and batted .308. Sorrento was added to the Twins' playoff roster by manager Tom Kelly. Although he saw limited action, he was part of the Twins' second world championship team in four years.

Sorrento was traded to Cleveland from Minnesota on March 28, 1992 for pitchers Oscar Múñoz and Curt Leskanic and was inserted as Cleveland's starting first baseman that season.

Sorrento wore a Tribe uniform for four seasons (1991–95) before moving on to Seattle (1996–97) and ending his career with the expansion Tampa Bay Devil Rays (1998–99). For his career, he belted 166 home runs, drove in 565 runs, batted .257, and was a dependable defensive player at first base.

Sorrento is currently the Los Angeles Angels assistant hitting coach. He also served as their minor league hitting coordinator (2013–15).

11. Kevin Millwood is the pitcher who was lacking run support in 2005.

Millwood, a native of Gastonia, North Carolina, was an 11th-round pick by the Atlanta Braves in 1993. He made his major-league debut on July 14, 1997, receiving credit for the victory after pitching two innings of relief against Philadelphia. At Triple-A Richmond in 1997, Millwood posted a 7–0 record with a 1.93 ERA, as he was shuttled back to the minors for three weeks in August after being called up in July.

Millwood became a mainstay in the Atlanta rotation. Three other members of the Braves staff were Hall of Fame worthy, including Tom Glavine, John Smoltz, and Greg Maddux. Millwood posted a 17–8 mark in 1998 and an 18–7 record in 1999. He won a game in both the NLDS against Houston and the NLCS against the New York Mets in 1999. However, Milwood was roughed up by the New York Yankees in Game Two of the World Series, giving up five runs (four earned) in only two innings.

After going 18–8 with a 3.24 ERA for Atlanta in 2002, he was traded to Philadelphia in the offseason. He pitched a no-hitter against the Giants on April 27, 2003. In 2004, Millwood experienced elbow problems and missed six weeks. He signed a one-year deal with Cleveland on January 8, 2005.

Cleveland had a 93–69 record in 2005 but could never catch the White Sox. Chicago won the AL Central in 2005 and dominated the Indians in head-to-head games, taking 14 of 19 matchups. Cleveland had a chance to make the playoffs but was swept at home by Chicago in the last series of the season.

The first game of that series was Millwood's season in a nutshell. Needing a win, Millwood surrendered one run in seven innings, striking out nine. Chicago won the game, 3–2, in 13 innings.

Millwood received 3.62 runs in offensive support per outing. Cliff Lee, who went 18–5, received 6.37 runs per outing. CC Sabathia, who won 15 games, received 5.05 runs per game.

Millwood moved on to Texas, where he won 16 games the following year. But his ERA continued to balloon in subsequent seasons as he pitched for various teams. He retired after 16 seasons in the big leagues with a career record of 169–152 and a 4.11 ERA. An excellent control pitcher, Millwood totaled 2,083 strikeouts while walking 843.

12. Bob Feller and Sam McDowell are the only two pitchers to record 2,000 or more strikeouts as a member of the Cleveland Indians.

The Indians were the only team that **Bob Feller** pitched for in his 18-year career. From 1942 to 1944 he served in World War II with the United States Navy. Feller was discharged late in 1945 and started only nine games that season.

Feller topped the 200-strikeout mark four times from 1938 to 1941. In each of those seasons he led the American

League in strikeouts. In 1946, Feller struck out 348, which is the fourth-highest total in AL history. Feller also led the league that year in wins (26), starts (42), complete games (36), shutouts (10), and innings pitched (371 1/3). Feller's ERA in 1946 was 2.18, third lowest in the league.

Feller finished his career with a record of 266–162 with a 3.25 ERA. He collected 2,581 strikeouts, 44 shutouts, and 279 complete games. He was a first-ballot selection to the Hall of Fame in 1962, garnering 93.8 percent of the votes.

Sam McDowell pitched for Cleveland from 1961 to 1970. "Sudden Sam" did not become part of the Indians rotation on a full-time basis until 1964. He surpassed the 300-strikeout total twice. In 1965, he posted 325 strikeouts (and he led the league with a 2.18 ERA), and in 1970, he whiffed 304 batters. Both times he led the league. Four other times he totaled more than 200 strikeouts, and in three of those years, he led the circuit. In 1970, McDowell went 20–12 with a 2.92 ERA. He led the league in strikeouts and innings pitched (305). He was named American League Pitcher of the Year by *The Sporting News* in 1970.

The 1970 season was the only one in his career that McDowell won 20 games. He was victimized by poor hitting clubs when he pitched in Cleveland. The Indians batted .250 as a team in 1965, which was the highest during McDowell's tenure. In his eight years as a starter, Cleveland's composite team batting average was .241.

Alcoholism led McDowell to his poor performance on the field and his erratic behavior off the field. He was traded after the 1971 season to San Francisco for Gaylord Perry and Frank Duffy. It remains one of the greatest trades in Indians history.

Sam McDowell was one of the fastest pitchers in team and league history. "I like Sudden, and I think he's got the greatest fastball, curveball, slider, and changeup I ever saw," said Reggie Jackson. "And he won't throw at you, either, because he's too nice a guy. He knows that with his fastball he could kill you if he ever hit you." *Courtesy of Cleveland Public Library/Photograph Collection.*

McDowell was released by the Pittsburgh Pirates in 1975, and he never pitched in the big leagues again. In his 11 years with the Indians, he posted a 122–109 record with a 2.99 ERA. He totaled 2,159 strikeouts.

McDowell beat his addictions. After his baseball career, he became a successful counselor and advised other professional sports teams and players who suffered from alcohol or drug addiction.

13. Andre Thornton drove in 105 runs in 1978 as well as 116 runs in 1982.

Thornton was signed as a non-drafted free agent by Philadelphia on August 6, 1967. He showed some power in the minor leagues as he belted 26 round-trippers for Double-A Reading in 1971. Nonetheless, he was traded to the Atlanta Braves on June 15, 1972. On May 19, 1973, the Braves dealt Thornton to the Chicago Cubs for Joe Pepitone. Thornton reported to Triple-A Wichita of the American Association. In 40 games for the Aeros, he belted 17 home runs and collected 45 RBIs. He earned a call-up to the Cubs, making his major-league debut on July 28, 1973.

Thornton started the majority of games at first base for the Cubs in 1974. In 1975, he led the team in home runs with 18, drove in 60 runs, and batted .293. But when Thornton got off to a slow start in 1976, he was dealt to Montreal on May 17. He was back on the bench for the Expos, spelling Mike Jorgenson at first base and playing some right field.

Cleveland acquired Thornton from the Expos in exchange for pitcher Jackie Brown on December 10, 1976. It was truly one of the greatest trades made by Phil Seghi in his time as Cleveland's general manager (1973–85).

Thornton found a home in Cleveland, and he would settle into an Indians uniform for the next 11 years. His impact was immediately felt as he led the team in home runs (28) and was second in RBIs (70) in 1977. Baltimore pitcher Jim Palmer revealed the strategy that he and many other pitchers around the league followed when facing Thornton. "When I face Cleveland, I just want to be able to pitch around Thornton. He'll turn my 1–0 win into a 2–1 loss."

On October 17, 1977, tragedy hit the Thornton family hard. Andre, his wife Gertrude, and their two children, Theresa and Andre Jr., were traveling to West Chester, Pennsylvania, for a wedding when a sudden snowstorm and high winds pushed the family van across the icy road and flipped it over into a ditch on the Pennsylvania Turnpike. Theresa was sleeping in her mother's arms in the front seat, while Andre Jr. was in the back seat. At the hospital, Andre learned that Gertrude and Theresa lost their lives while Andre Jr. had survived the crash. Thornton remarried in 1979 to the former Gail Ellen Jones of Chicago. They had two sons together, Dean and Jonathon.

Andre Thornton was the big bat in the Cleveland lineup through many lean years in the late 1970s through mid 1980s. He is one of only eight players in franchise history to hit for the cycle—April 22, 1978 at Boston's Fenway Park.
Courtesy of Cleveland Public Library/Photograph Collection.

Thornton missed the entire 1980 season due to a knee injury he suffered in spring training. He rebounded from the injury and the strike-shortened 1981 season to have his best year in 1982. He had 161 hits, smacked 32 home runs, drove in 116 runs, and batted .273. Thornton was named as *The Sporting News* Comeback Player of the Year. He was rewarded with his first All-Star Game selection and was also selected to the midsummer classic in 1984. "All I needed was my health," said Thornton. "If I could stay sound, I knew I could produce. Just check my record. If I don't get hurt, I can put up some good numbers. To me, this season was gratifying, but it certainly didn't shock me."

When Cleveland acquired Mike Hargrove from San Diego in 1979, he moved from the outfield to take Thornton's spot at first in 1980. Thornton was relegated to designated hitter for the most part of the remainder of his career. He was named the winner of the Silver Slugger Award in 1984 when he led all DHs with 33 home runs. In the 10 seasons that Thornton saw action in Cleveland, he hit 214 home runs, drove in 749 runs, and totaled 193 doubles. He batted .254 while he was a member of the Indians. His 214 home runs as an Indian rank him seventh all-time on the team's all-time list.

He was the first Cleveland player to be awarded the Roberto Clemente Award in 1979. The award is named after the Pittsburgh Pirates great and honors those who "best exemplify baseball, sportsmanship, community involvement, and the individual's contribution to his team."

Thornton retired after the 1987 season after 14 years in the big leagues. He clubbed 253 home runs and collected 895 RBIs. His lifetime batting average was .254. Thornton has hit the most home runs in Cleveland Stadium history with 119.

As of 2018, Andre Thornton is the CEO and chairman of ASW Global, a supply chain management company based in Mogadore, Ohio.

14. Gene Bearden, a rookie pitcher in 1948, won Game Three of the 1948 World Series. Bearden also went 2-for-3 at the plate with a double and a run scored. In the history of Cleveland Stadium, Bearden and Steve Gromek are the only Cleveland pitchers credited with a win in World Series competition.

Bearden was born in Lexa, Arkansas, on September 5, 1920. Ironically, he was born the same year Cleveland won its first World Series. His baseball career might never have happened at all, as Bearden was aboard the *USS Helena* in the South Pacific where it was battling the Japanese near the Solomon Islands. The ship was under attack by the Japanese as it was struck with three torpedoes on July 6, 1943. Out of a crew of about 900, 168 perished as the ship sank. Bearden was found adrift in a life raft, his head badly smashed open and with a torn up knee.

Bearden was hospitalized for two years as a steel plate was inserted in his skull and a hinge was placed in his knee. His injuries affected him for the rest of his life, as he had to take painkillers and his vision suffered.

Bearden was originally signed by the Philadelphia Phillies in 1939. He went 18–10 with a 1.63 ERA for Miami Beach in the Class D Florida East Coast League in 1940. Bearden returned to Miami Beach in 1941 and pitched well, going 17–7 with a 2.40 ERA. He was sold to the New York Yankees in 1942, but his season was cut short so he could report to the Great Lakes Naval Training Center for basic training and machinist school.

After his recuperation, Bearden returned to baseball after his discharge in 1945. It was a miracle that he could return to the diamond at all, but Bearden won 15 games in the minor leagues each of the following two seasons. He was part of a five-player deal that sent him to Cleveland on December 26, 1946.

He made one appearance for the Indians on May 10, 1947, but spent the remaining season with Oakland of the Pacific Coast League, where he won 16 games. He made the Cleveland roster in 1948, making his first start on May 8, at Washington's Griffith Stadium. Bearden pitched the Indians to a 6–1 victory over the Senators.

Bearden was a left-handed knuckleball pitcher, and in 1948, he made 29 starts for the Tribe. At times he could master the knuckler. But still, his walks outnumbered his strikeouts, 106 to 80. The Indians ended up in a tie with the Boston Red Sox. Indians manager Lou Boudreau tapped Bearden to start the one-game playoff at Fenway Park on October 4. The Indians won the game, 8–3, as Bearden notched his 20th victory. He posted a 20–7 record and led the American League with a 2.43 ERA.

In addition to winning Game Three of the World Series, Bearden also earned a save in Game Six at Braves Field. He relieved Bob Lemon in the top of the eighth inning with Cleveland leading, 4–1. The Braves had the bases loaded and one out. The Braves scored two more times to make the score 4–3. Bearden recorded three outs in the ninth inning to give Cleveland their second world championship.

But Bearden would never duplicate the success he had in 1948. He had a splendid knuckler but little else. Cleveland waived him in 1950, and he later pitched for Washington, Detroit, the St. Louis Browns, and the Chicago White Sox. He pitched for seven seasons and had a lifetime record of 45–38 with a 3.96 ERA. He totaled 259 strikeouts, but he walked 435 batters.

Despite the injuries he sustained in World War II, Bearden lived a long life. He passed away from congestive heart failure on March 18, 2004, at the age of eighty-three.

15. The three players who were wearing Cleveland threads while reaching the 3,000 hit milestone were:

Nap Lajoie (3,243 hits)—September 27, 1914 at League Park

Tris Speaker (3,514 hits)—May 17, 1925 at Dunn Field

Eddie Murray (3,255 hits)—June 30, 1995 at Hubert H. Humphrey Metrodome, Minneapolis.

Nap Lajoie was born on September 5, 1874 in Woonsocket, Rhode Island. After knocking around with semipro teams near his hometown, Lajoie was signed by Fall River of the New England League in 1896. Word spread of his talent with both the glove and bat. The Philadelphia Phillies purchased Lajoie for $1,500 that same year. He wasted little time in demonstrating his offensive prowess. He batted .326 in 39 games for the Phillies in 1896. Incredibly, in 16 of the next 18 seasons, Lajoie batted over .300. After a salary dispute with the Phillies front office, Lajoie jumped ship to join the Philadelphia Athletics of the newly formed American League in 1901. Phillies owner John Rogers sought to block this move in getting an injunction to prohibit Lajoie from playing professional baseball in the state of Pennsylvania.

Even though he batted .426 for the Athletics in 1901, Lajoie was granted free agency. He wouldn't be much good to the Athletics to appear in only road games. Cleveland was the next stop for Lajoie, where he remained through 1914.

In 13 seasons with the team, Lajoie ranks second in games (1,614), first in at-bats (6,034), first in hits (2,047), second in doubles (424), third in total bases (2,725), third in RBIs (919), fourth in steals (240), and third in batting average (.340). His lifetime batting average of .338 ties him for 18th of all-time with Jesse Burkett and Tony Gwynn. Lajoie led the league in various offensive and defensive categories multiple seasons including doubles four times, batting average and hits four times, RBIs three times, and home runs and runs once. In the field, Lajoie led the AL in fielding percentage and double plays six times, putouts five times, and assists three times. He fielded his second base position at a .963 clip in 2,035 games.

The Cleveland Bronchos of 1902 became known as the Cleveland Naps, in honor of Lajoie. Lajoie became the manager of the club, succeeding Bill Armour in 1905. Lajoie was the skipper until 1909, compiling a record of 377–309 for a winning percentage of .550.

Lajoie was elected to the Hall of Fame in 1937. He passed away on February 7, 1959, after a bout with pneumonia.

Tris Speaker was born in Hubbard, Texas, on April 4, 1888. Although he was a pitcher in high school, Speaker did not fare so well on the mound in professional baseball. Signed by Class D Cleburne of the Texas League, Speaker lost six consecutive games. The Texas League and South Texas League merged, and Speaker moved on to Class C Houston in 1907 where he led the league with a .314 batting average.

His contract was purchased by the Boston Red Sox in 1907, but appeared in only seven games, batting .158. He was not offered a contract the following year, and Speaker paid his own way to Boston's spring training home in Little Rock,

Nicknamed "Larry," Nap Lajoie was not only a great hitter, but swift in the field too. "He plays so naturally and so easily it looks like lack of effort," Connie Mack would observe. "Larry's reach is so long and he's fast as lightning, and to throw to at second base he is ideal. All the catchers who've played with him say he is the easiest man to throw to in the game today. High, low, wide—he is sure of everything."
Harris & Ewing Collection (Library of Congress) via Wikimedia Commons.

Arkansas. Boston sold Speaker to Little Rock with the condition that if he developed, Boston could purchase him back for $500.

Speaker led the Southern Association in batting with a .350 average and stole 28 bases in 1908. As planned, Speaker was sold back to the Red Sox. Although he batted a weak .224 in 31 games in 1908, his defense in center field was astounding. He covered a lot of territory, seemingly with ease.

Boston won two world championships while Speaker was a member of the Red Sox, 1912 and 1915. From 1909 to 1915, Speaker never batted below .300, and he led the league in home runs (10) and doubles (53) in 1912.

A contract squabble with the Red Sox landed Speaker in Cleveland, as he was traded to the Indians on April 9, 1916, for two players and $55,000. Speaker, who was a member of the Indians from 1916 to 1926, led the AL in doubles six times. For his career, Speaker is the major leagues' all-time leader in doubles with 792. After 11 seasons with the Indians, Speaker appears at the top of many offensive categories in franchise history. He ranks fifth in games (1,519), second in runs (1,079), second in hits (1,965), first in doubles (486), second in triples (108), second in total bases (2,886), fifth in RBIs (886), second in walks (857), and second in batting average (.354). His lifetime batting average of .345 ranks him sixth all-time in major-league history. Speaker fielded his center field position at a .970 clip over 22 seasons.

He took over for Lee Fohl as the Cleveland manager midway through the 1919 season. He continued his dual responsibilities as player-manager through 1926. His career record was 617–520 for a .543 winning percentage. He led Cleveland to their first world championship in 1920 when the Indians beat Brooklyn in seven games. His 617 victories rank him third among Cleveland managers behind Lou Boudreau (728) and Mike Hargrove (721). He moved on to the Washington Senators in 1927 and finished his career with the Philadelphia Athletics a year later.

Tris Speaker was elected to the Hall of Fame in 1937. He passed away on December 8, 1958, as the result of a heart attack.

Eddie Murray was born February 24, 1956 in Los Angeles California. He was selected by Baltimore in the third round of the amateur draft in 1973 and ascended through the Orioles farm system. In 1976, he batted .289 with 23 home runs and 86 RBIs between Double-A Charlotte of the Southern League and Triple-A Rochester of the International League.

Murray won a job with Baltimore in 1977. He batted .283, swatted 27 home runs, and drove in 88 runs. He was named the American League Rookie of the Year by the Baseball Writers Association of America. From 1977 to 1988, Murray was a model of consistency with the Orioles. He was awarded the Gold Glove three consecutive seasons (1982–84) for his excellence in fielding from his first base position and was selected to the AL All-Star team five consecutive years (1981–85). He was the member of two pennant-winning teams (1979, 1983) and one world championship team in 1983.

After 1988, Murray moved over to the National League. He was a member of the Los Angeles Dodgers (1989–91) and the New York Mets (1992–93).

He signed with Cleveland as a free agent on December 2, 1993. Murray brought instant credibility and leadership in the clubhouse. He shared time at first base with Paul Sorrento and also served as a designated hitter. In 309 games over three seasons with the Indians, he batted .281 with 50 home runs and 203 RBIs.

Murray returned to Baltimore in 1996. His last season was in 1997, which was split between the Dodgers and Anaheim Angels. In 21 seasons and 3,026 games, Murray smashed 504 home runs, collected 1,917 RBIs, and batted .287. He fielded his first base position at a .993 percentage in 2,413 games. After his playing days, he was the Indians' hitting coach from 2002 to 2005.

Murray was elected to the Hall of Fame in 2003.

16. The Cleveland Indians' starting pitcher in Game Six of the 1920 World Series, John Walter Mails, certainly did not have an issue with his confidence. "Brooklyn will be lucky to get a foul off me today. If Spoke [Cleveland player-manager Tris Speaker] and the boys will give me one run, Cleveland will win," said Mails. He was commonly referred to as Duster Mails, a moniker given to him for the occasional brushback pitches he would hurl at batters. Mails preferred to be called The Great Mails, and his 1920 regular-season record would certainly give credence to that preference.

Mails was a former member of the Robins. He broke into professional baseball with the Class B Seattle Giants of the Northwestern League in 1914. The next year Mails was still pitching for Seattle, where he was 24–18 with 250 strikeouts in 348 innings of work. Brooklyn bought his contract, but he was seldom used in his two seasons in Flatbush.

Cleveland acquired Mails from Sacramento of the Pacific Coast League on August 21, 1920. He was recommended to Indians manager Tris Speaker by Frank Chance. The former great first baseman had seen Mails pitch while managing in the PCL and declared that Mails was the best left-handed hurler in the PCL, or any baseball league for that matter.

Mails lived up to the lofty billing, posting a 7–0 record between September 1 and October 1 with a 1.85 ERA. One of his key performances came on September 24, when he shut out the White Sox on a three-hitter, 2–0. The victory pushed Cleveland to a 1 1/2-game lead over Chicago with the regular season coming down to the wire. That he outdueled Red Faber, who had won 23 games that year, in such a crucial game made his feat even more astounding.

Mails was opposed in Game Six by Sherry Smith. The left-handed Smith (11–9, 1.85 ERA in the regular season) was the winner of Game Three when he went the distance, scattering three hits and striking out two in the Robins' 2–1 win. Sure enough, Mails did as he said he would, scattering three hits as he shut out Brooklyn, 1–0. The win put the Indians on the verge of winning the first world championship in franchise history.

Although Mails went 14–8 in 1921, he was not able to duplicate the success he had in 1920. In seven seasons in the major leagues, Mails was 32–25 and posted a 4.10 ERA. He totaled 232 strikeouts and 220 walks. He returned to the Pacific Coast League, where he pitched until 1936.

Mails passed away on July 5, 1974 as the result of prostate cancer, heart disease, and Parkinson's disease.

17. Wayne Kirby singled home Eddie Murray with the winning run in the bottom of the 11th inning, giving the Tribe a 4–3 victory over the Mariners in the first game played at Jacobs Field. With one down, Murray doubled to center field and advanced to third base when Paul Sorrento flied out. Sandy Alomar Jr. was intentionally walked. Kirby sliced a 3-1 pitch from Seattle reliever Kevin King to left field for a single, scoring Murray.

Cleveland celebrated a rebirth of their baseball franchise in 1994. The new configuration of the divisions helped, as they were now in a five-team AL Central instead of in the old AL East. The season ended on August 12, 1994, due to a player's strike. But the fans got a taste of the good life, with an open-air, baseball-only stadium. They finished the season with a 66–47 record, just one game behind the Chicago White Sox.

Wayne Kirby was a 13th round pick by the Los Angeles Dodgers in the January 1983 amateur draft. He scuttled around their minor-league system for eight years, but could not break through to the majors. Kirby was granted free agency by the Dodgers on October 15, 1990 and signed with Cleveland two months later. He split the next two seasons between Cleveland and their Triple-A affiliate in Colorado Springs.

In 1993, he earned a starting spot in right field. But the emergence of Manny Ramirez put Kirby on the pine. He returned to the Dodgers on June 24, 1996 after being waived by the Indians. He played for the Dodgers (1996–97) and the New York Mets (1998) before retiring. In 516 major-league games, Kirby batted .252 with 14 home runs, 119 RBIs, and 183 runs.

After his playing days, Kirby kept himself active in professional baseball. He was a minor-league hitting instructor with Cleveland (2002–05), and he served as an outfield and baserunning coach in the Texas system (2006–10). Kirby completed his seventh season as the first-base coach of the Baltimore Orioles in 2017.

18. Bill Selby homered off Mariano Rivera to cap the comeback against the New York Yankees.

The Yankees had jumped out to an early lead, scoring seven runs off Cleveland starter Chuck Finley in just 3 1/3 innings. But a three-run homer by Jim Thome in the sixth inning and a single run in the seventh frame shaved the Yankees advantage to 7–4 going into the bottom of the ninth.

The rally began when John McDonald and Eddie Pérez both singled to put runners on the corners. Chris McGruder hit a comebacker to Rivera, who got the lead runner at second base, but McGruder beat the return throw. McDonald scored on the play. Omar Vizquel followed with a single to right field, and McGruder raced to third. Ellis Burks doubled home McGruder, and Vizquel checked in at third base. Thome was given an intentional free pass and then Rivera struck out pinch-hitter Travis Fryman for the second out. Selby came to the plate and hit Rivera's 2-2 cutter into the right-field stands for the game-winner. It was the first grand slam that Rivera had given up in 435 major-league appearances. "He hit my best pitch," Rivera said. "It was right there where I wanted it . . . a cutter moving in."

Bill Selby, the pride of Monroeville, Alabama, was selected by Boston in the 13th round of the amateur draft in 1992. Ironically, he made his major-league debut on April 19, 1996 at Jacobs Field.

But Selby was returned to Triple-A Pawtucket in 1996, and in 1997 Selby played in Japan for Yokohama. He signed on with Cleveland in 1998 and spent two seasons in the minors before making it to Cleveland in 2000. Perhaps he is best known for giving Travis Hafner his nickname, "Pronkey" (Part Project, Part Donkey), which was eventually shortened to "Pronk."

In five major-league seasons with Boston, Cleveland, and Cincinnati, Selby appeared in 198 games, mostly at third base, batting .223 with 11 home runs and 48 RBIs.

19. Terry Turner has appeared in the most games wearing a Cleveland uniform. Turner played from 1904 to 1918 with the Cleveland Naps/Indians, playing 1,619 games. Turner's former teammate, Napoleon Lajoie, is right behind him with 1,614 games played.

Turner, who was from Sandy Lake, Pennsylvania, started his career playing in a couple of amateur leagues. First it was the Wheeling Stogies of the Interstate League and then Ashtabula (Ohio) of the Iron and Oil League. Turner, who was 5-foot-8 and 148 pounds, was on the small side. But he was aggressive on the basepaths and swung a fair bat. He drew some interest from big-league clubs and signed with Pittsburgh in 1901, but he got into only two games.

The Pirates released him to Class A Columbus of the American Association, where he settled in at shortstop for two seasons. He batted .293 in 1902 while also stealing 41 bases and then hit .310 in 1903. He also developed the head-first slide. "I discovered at Columbus that sliding feet-first wasn't for me," said Turner. "I caught my spikes too often and hurt my ankles. Yes, I suppose head-first was dangerous, too, and I still have scars on my hands where I got stepped on. But for me, it was better."

This period of professional baseball is referred to as the "Deadball Era" or the "Inside Game." Runs were manufactured using sacrifice bunts, hitting behind the runner, and squeeze plays. The home run was not yet in vogue. This brand of baseball was a natural fit for Turner. "Inside work is a big factor in modern baseball," said Turner. "You will observe, if you look closely, that winning teams are the ones that have developed this feature of the game. Inside work does not permit individual playing as much as where every man is a unit, but it brings results, and, after all, that is what counts."

Although Turner was a shortstop by trade, he adapted well to second and third base as well. "The most valuable infielder in the American League . . . as he can play third base, second base, and shortstop equally well," said Naps manager Joe Birmingham. "It is only once in a lifetime that you find one of these players who is brilliant wherever you play him . . . He is too valuable a man to tie at one position when he is so good at several."

He had a bout with typhoid fever in 1904, and he was hit by a pitch in 1908 that crushed in his skull, and it was remarkable that he lived, much less continued playing baseball.

Turner ranks high among the leaders on Cleveland's all-time lists. He is tenth in hits (1,472), third in stolen bases (254), and ninth in triples (77). His batting average while with Cleveland was .254.

In retirement, Turner worked as a chief superintendent at the City of Cleveland Street Department. He passed away on July 18, 1960 as the result of a stroke.

20. Doug Jones preserved the 5–3 American League victory by pitching 1 1/3 scoreless innings.

Jones was originally drafted out of Central Arizona College in January 1978 by the Milwaukee Brewers. Jones initially began his career as a starting pitcher but was relegated to the bullpen. He was not an overpowering pitcher, and in some vernacular he would be known as an "off-speed pitcher." Jones pitched in the Brewers' farm system with limited success. He kept batters off balance with a tremendous changeup instead of throwing smoke like traditional closers.

He made four appearances with Milwaukee in 1982, but he was released in October 1984. Jones signed with the Indians on April 3, 1985. From 1988 to 1990 he was one of the best relievers in the major leagues, totaling 112 saves over those three years. He was selected to the American League All-Star team all three seasons. He possessed excellent control, striking out 192 batters while walking 51 during this time period. Jones had a disastrous 1991 season, as his saves total shrank to seven and his ERA jumped from 2.56 in 1990 to 5.54. He was demoted to Triple-A Colorado Springs and was designated for assignment at the end of the 1991 season.

Jones signed with Houston, and he was spectacular. He posted an 11–8 record with a 1.85 ERA to go along with 36 saves in 1992. Jones led the Astros, who finished with a .500 record at 81–81, in wins and saves, a true anomaly. He was named to the NL All-Star team and *The Sporting News* NL Fireman of the Year.

Jones pitched for several teams over the next several years, including Houston (1992–93), Philadelphia (1994), Baltimore (1995), Chicago Cubs (1996), Milwaukee (1996–98), Cleveland (1998), and Oakland (1999–2000).

In 16 seasons, Jones saved 303 games, which ranks him 25th all-time as of 2017. He ranks second in Cleveland Indians history in saves (129) to Bob Wickman (139).

In retirement, Jones worked with the Arizona Diamondbacks as a special assistant in their minor league department (2006–08). He spent four seasons as a pitching coach for San Diego Christian College (2009–14).

Jones joined the Colorado Rockies organization as a minor league pitching coach. As of 2017, he was the pitching coach for the Grand Junction Rockies, a rookie league team in the Pioneer League.

21. Paul Dade was sent to San Diego in exchange for Hargrove.

Dade was drafted in the first round (10th overall) by the California Angels in the June 1970 amateur draft. He toiled in the Angels farm system for a few years before making his major-league debut on September 12, 1975. However, the Angels made a deal to acquire Bobby Bonds from the New York Yankees in the offseason. The addition of Bonds cut into Dade's projected playing time. When the Angels added Don Baylor and Joe Rudi via free agency after 1976, Dade was the odd man out.

Dade signed with the Indians on February 10, 1977. He was looking for a fresh start and a better opportunity. But although he showed some competency at the plate and in the field, he was platooned by manager Frank Robinson. When Jeff Torborg replaced Robinson in 1977, he used Dade much in the same manner.

Cleveland acquired Bobby Bonds from Texas in the off-season, and Bonds was given the right field job in 1979. Dade again was relegated to the bench and was then traded to the Padres. "Up until a few weeks ago, I wanted to be traded," Dade confessed. "[But] I started getting hot at the plate and playing regularly and the team started winning. . . . I hate to leave it."

Dade was installed as the third baseman in San Diego, but again, his playing time was curtailed. In his six years in the majors, Dade batted .270 with 10 home runs and 107 RBIs.

After his playing days, he had a twenty-seven-year career as a machine operator for a box-making company outside of his hometown in Seattle. Dade passed away from kidney cancer on August 25, 2016.

Mike Hargrove broke in with the Texas Rangers in 1974. He was installed as the starting first baseman by Texas manager Billy Martin, and he responded well to the challenge. "Grover" batted .323 with four home runs and 66 RBIs. Hargrove was voted the American League Rookie of the Year by the Baseball Writers Association of America and *The Sporting News*.

Hargrove was a productive first baseman for the Rangers and was an on-base threat. Twice he led the AL in walks with the Rangers. In 1978, his batting average dipped to .251 from .305 in 1977. Hargrove was included in a five-player deal that sent him west to San Diego on October 25, 1978.

Hargrove proved to be a steady player for Cleveland and solidified the first base position for years. Although he lacked speed, Hargrove walked often and was a contact hitter who got on base. Hargrove played from 1979 to 1985 in Cleveland, batting .292 and totaling 505 walks. Hargrove posted a .424 on-base percentage in 1981, which led the American League. He ranks ninth in franchise history in on-base percentage with .396.

After his career, Hargrove managed in the Indians farm system until 1990 when he joined John McNamara's staff in Cleveland. He replaced McNamara on July 6, 1991 and was the Indians' manager through 1999. He led the team to five division championships (1995–99) and two pennants (1995, 1997). His 721 wins are second in Cleveland Indian's history to Lou Boudreau (728). He was named AL Manager of the Year by *The Sporting News* in 1995.

Hargrove later managed in Baltimore (2000–03) and Seattle (2005–07). His managerial record is 1,183–1,165 for a .504 winning percentage.

22. Bob Lemon is the Indians pitcher who has a career mark of 2–2 in World Series competition. In 1948 against Boston, Lemon won Game Two on October 7 by a score of 4–1 and the world championship–clinching Game Six, 4–3, on October 11. Both games were at Braves Field.

In 1954 against New York, Lemon lost Game One on September 29 at the Polo Grounds, 5–2. He lost again on October 2 in Game Four at Cleveland Stadium, 7–4.

Bob Lemon hailed from San Bernardino, California, where he was signed out of high school by Cleveland in 1938. Although he signed for $100 a month as a pitcher, Lemon also had some "pop" in his bat. He showed his ability to hit the long ball, smacking 21 home runs and driving in 80 runs for Baltimore of the International League in 1942.

Lemon enlisted in the United States Navy as World War II broke out. He was stationed in California and Hawaii, playing on naval base teams. He flourished as one of the top players in armed services competition.

Lemon joined the Indians after he received his discharge. Manager Lou Boudreau had an abundance of pitching at his disposal, so he inserted Lemon in center field. But it soon became apparent that Lemon could not hit major-league pitching. "I could hit anything else they threw at me, but not the changeup, and the word got around pretty quick," said Lemon. "Pretty soon that's all I saw. Fastball out of the strike zone. Curveball out of the strike zone. Then the damned changeup."

Bob Lemon ranks third in franchise history in wins (207) and has more 20-win seasons to his credit than any Indians pitcher with seven.
Courtesy of Cleveland Public Library/Photograph Collection.

He was added to the pitching staff and a Hall of Fame career was born. Lemon won 20 or more games in seven seasons. Three times he led the league in wins. On June 30, 1948,

Lemon threw a no-hitter against the Detroit Tigers. That same year, he put together scoreless streaks of 29 innings (May 20 to June 2) and 31 innings (August 25 to September 8). He was honored by *The Sporting News* three times as the paper's American League Pitcher of the Year (1948, 1950, and 1954). His career record was 207–128 with a 3.23 ERA.

Lemon managed in Kansas City (1970–1972), Chicago White Sox (1977–78), and the New York Yankees (1978–79, 1981–82). He won one world championship with the Yankees (1978). His career managerial record was 430–403 for a .516 winning percentage.

Lemon was inducted into the Hall of Fame in 1976. He passed away on January 11, 2000, as the result of a heart attack after he suffered a series of strokes.

23. CC Sabathia was the Tribe pitcher who went yard twice. He hit a home run in the following games:

May 21, 2005 at Great American Ballpark, Cincinnati

June 21, 2008 at Dodger Stadium, Los Angeles

Sabathia, 6-foot-7 and a left-handed batter, was one pitcher who liked to step into the batter's box. While he was in the National League with Milwaukee in 2008, Sabathia batted .229 (11-for-48), which is exceptional for a pitcher. He hit a home run on July 13 at Miller Park to give him three for his career. Sabathia also drove in six runs in his brief time with the Brewers.

The other three Cleveland pitchers who have hit home runs post–interleague play are:

Dave Burba—June 7, 1998 at Cinergy Field, Cincinnati

Dwight Gooden—June 11, 1999 at Cinergy Field, Cincinnati

Jason Davis—June 20, 2004 at Turner Field, Atlanta

24. In 1962, John Romano led Cleveland with 25 home runs and 81 RBIs.

In 2007, Víctor Martínez was the Indians' starting catcher and he also hit 25 home runs. However, three of those came while he was playing first base. In 2011, Carlos Santana was the starting catcher for the Tribe, and he belted 27 round-trippers. However, nine of those homers came as a first baseman and one as a pinch-hitter.

Romano, who hailed from Hoboken, New Jersey, was signed as an amateur free agent by the Chicago White Sox in 1954. Romano was a catcher from the very beginning of his professional career. However, it was not until 1958 when former major-league catcher Walker Cooper helped him to hone his craft. "When I first went down to the minor leagues," said Romano, "I played for about two or three years for former infielders as managers. [Then] the White Sox sent down Walker Cooper to manage their Triple-A team. He was the backup catcher, plus he was the manager. When Cooper came down there [to Indianapolis], he straightened me out. The White Sox said the only thing that was holding me back from not going to the big leagues was not knowing how to catch. Walker Cooper helped me very much in that regard."

Romano had no trouble swinging the lumber. But under Cooper's tutelage he became more of a complete player. He was a late-season call-up to the White Sox in 1958. The following season he served as a backup to Sherman Lollar on the White Sox's pennant-winning team in 1959.

But Chicago had a surplus of young talent, and Romano was included in a seven-player deal with Cleveland on December 6, 1959. Over the next five seasons with the Indians, Romano blossomed into one of the better backstops in the

American League. In 580 games as an Indian, he belted 91 home runs and drove in 294 runs while batting .263. He was selected to the AL All-Star team in 1961 and 1962. "It wasn't a popularity contest in those years," said Romano. "Each ball-player had one vote. Those guys are the ones that voted me in as the catcher. It was the actual baseball players that played against me that voted for me, and getting voted in by your peers was a big honor. You look today and most of it is just a popularity contest."

Romano was traded back to the White Sox on January 20, 1965 as part of a three-team swap between Cleveland, Chicago, and Kansas City. He was the regular catcher for Chicago in 1965 and 1966. His last year in the majors was in 1967, when he appeared in 20 games for St. Louis. In 10 seasons and 905 games in the big leagues, Romano clubbed 129 homers, collected 417 RBIs, and batted .255.

25. In 1953, Al Rosen was the last Cleveland Indian to be named Most Valuable Player by the BWAA. Rosen just missed the Triple Crown as he led the American League in home runs (43) and RBIs (145). However, his .336 batting average was second to Washington's Mickey Vernon's average of .337. Rosen had also led the AL in runs (115) in 1953.

Rosen, a native of Spartanburg, Georgia, attended the University of Florida for two years before signing with the Indians in 1942. After one season at Class D Thomasville in 1942, Rosen enlisted in the United States Navy. He was discharged with the rank of lieutenant and was assigned to the Class C Pittsfield Electrics, batting .323 with 15 home runs.

Rosen, a third baseman, had his path to the major leagues blocked by Ken Keltner. Over the next three seasons, Rosen got a taste of major-league action, as he was mostly a late season call-up by the Tribe from 1947 to 1949. In 1950, with Keltner aging, the hot corner was turned over to Rosen. For the next seven seasons, he was one of the top third baseman in the major leagues. His defense was just as stellar as his offense. Rosen became a fan favorite and was a selection for the American League All-Star team four straight years (1952–55).

His lifetime batting average was .285. Rosen hammered 192 home runs and collected 717 RBIs. Rosen fielded his third base position at a .961 clip and led the AL in assists twice (1950 and 1953).

After his career ended, Rosen spent seventeen years as a stockbroker in Cleveland. He left in 1973 for a job at Caesar's Palace in Las Vegas. After five years, he was lured back to baseball by New York Yankees owner George Steinbrenner. Rosen was named president and CEO in 1978.

As might be expected, Rosen's tenure in New York was tumultuous. Dealing with Steinbrenner and Billy Martin was no picnic, and Rosen resigned a year and a half later. Rosen also held front office positions with the Houston Astros and San Francisco Giants. He was honored as the Major League Executive of the Year by *The Sporting News* in 1987 while with the Giants.

Rosen passed away on March 13, 2015 from natural causes.

3

ALL-STAR LEVEL

ALL-STAR LEVEL

(Answers begin on page 105)

1. Which Cleveland Indian player led the team in home runs during the decade of the 1960s?

2. On August 29, 1977, at Cleveland Stadium, Duane Kuiper hit the only home run in his career. Who was the opposing pitcher who gave up the round-tripper?

3. In Game Five of the 1920 World Series, the Indians were responsible for three "firsts" in series history. What were these feats?

4. Kenny Lofton holds four of the five spots in the Top 5 list for stolen bases in a season for the Tribe. Who holds the fourth highest total?

5. Two players in Cleveland history, one for the Naps and one for the Spiders, each hit over .400 in a season. Who were these accomplished batters?

6. On both August 13, 1916 and on August 19, 2016, the Cleveland Indians won a game courtesy of a walk-off, inside-the-park home run. Who were the two players who accomplished the feat and who are linked together after 100 years?

7. On October 28, 1995, the Atlanta Braves defeated the Cleveland Indians, 1–0, in Game Six of the World Series. The victory gave the Braves franchise their first world championship since moving from Milwaukee in 1966.

Tom Glavine pitched eight innings and only surrendered one hit. Which Indian got the hit off Glavine?

8. On July 31, 1963 at Cleveland Stadium, the Indians hit four consecutive home runs in one inning against the Los Angeles Angels. Who were the four players that went yard for the Tribe?

9. Who are the four players that have hit more than 40 career home runs for both the Cleveland Indians and the New York Yankees?

10. On March 30, 1978, Cleveland traded Dennis Eckersley and Fred Kendall to Boston for which four players?

11. There have been seven pitchers who at one time in their career pitched for the Cleveland Indians and subsequently went on to win a Cy Young Award for another team. Name these seven sterling moundsmen.

12. In 1962, *The Sporting News* selected this Indians hurler as their American League Pitcher of the Year. Who was he?

13. From 1973 to 1976 and again in 1978, Buddy Bell was the opening day third baseman for Cleveland. Who was the starting third baseman in 1977?

14. Who holds the longest hitting streak in Cleveland baseball history?

15. In the strike-shortened 1994 season, two Tribe pitchers tied for the team lead in wins with 11. Who were they?

16. On May 15, 1981, Len Barker pitched a perfect game against the Toronto Blue Jays at Cleveland Stadium.

Who was the first and only other hurler in Cleveland baseball history to throw a perfect game? It happened seventy-three years prior to Barker's gem.

17. On April 29, 1931, at League Park, this Indians pitcher twirled a no-hitter against the St. Louis Browns. The hurler backed the 9–0 victory with a home run and a double, knocking in four runs. Who was this Indians pitcher?

18. Which member of the Cleveland Indians' world championship team in 1920 went on to become an obstetrician after his career ended?

19. Two Indians pitchers have each strung together a streak of 15 wins in a row. Who were these two great Tribe pitchers?

20. On August 24, 1919, the Cleveland Indians were leading the Philadelphia Athletics, 2–1, at League Park. With two outs in the ninth inning, an impending storm exploded over the park. This Cleveland pitcher was struck by lightning and was knocked to the ground. The pitcher picked himself up and continued to pitch. Who was this electrifying Tribe pitcher?

21. Which Indians player did *The Sporting News* award as its Comeback Player of the Year in 1975?

22. Who hit the most career doubles at Cleveland Stadium?

23. Who hit the most career triples at Cleveland Stadium?

24. There are four members of the Hall of Fame who were each a member of the Cleveland Indians for only one

season. For each player, their one season with the Tribe was their last one in the major leagues. Name them.

25. This Indians player homered in his first major league at-bat on September 29, 1986, at the Hubert H. Humphrey Metrodome in Minneapolis. Name him.

ALL-STAR LEVEL — ANSWERS

1. Max Alvis led the Indians with 108 home runs from 1963 to 1969.

Alvis was a two-sport star at the University of Texas in the mid-1950s. During the fall he was a running back and linebacker for the Longhorns under legendary coach Darrell Royal. In the spring, he was the third baseman on Bibb Falk's baseball team.

He left Austin to join the Indians in 1959. He began his ascent, a climb that took four years, through the Cleveland farm system beginning at Class D Selma of the Alabama-Florida State League. Alvis was installed as the Tribe's starting third baseman in 1963, and he clubbed at least 17 round-trippers (99 total) each season from 1963 through 1967.

Alvis was diagnosed with spinal meningitis in June 1964. Although he returned to baseball later that season, his strength was weakening. "Max used to be the strongest player on the team," said teammate Vern Fuller. "Later, his skin color was different, more pale. He lost some of his muscle tone. He got tired much faster. He should have sat out the rest of the season." Alvis agreed with Fuller, "Before I got sick I worked hard, and I wasn't intimidated by anything. But when I came back I don't really think I had the brute strength that I'd had, and I couldn't regain it. [Meningitis] did something to my system. I never had any other effects that I know of, but I wasn't as strong as I'd been before."

Max Alvis was a solid performer at the hot corner in the 1960s for the Indians. Not only was he a home run threat, he led the club in doubles three different seasons.
Courtesy of Cleveland Public Library/Photograph Collection.

Cleveland traded for Graig Nettles after the 1969 season. Nettles was a star in the making, and he became the new starting third baseman. Alvis was traded to Milwaukee just before the 1970 season. It was the last season in professional baseball for Alvis, who retired after nine seasons with 111 home runs, 373 RBIs, and a .247 batting average.

2. Chicago White Sox right-hander Steve Stone was the victim of Kuiper's lone career home run.

Stone attended Brush High School in Lyndhurst, Ohio. After high school, Stone enrolled at Kent State University, where he was a teammate of Thurman Munson. Stone was originally drafted in 1968 by Cleveland, but he did not sign a contract. However, he did sign the following year after being drafted by San Francisco. Stone pitched for the Giants, Cubs, and White Sox and was mostly a .500 pitcher from 1971 through 1978. He signed as a free agent with Baltimore on November 29, 1978. Stone had a good year in 1979, as he posted an 11–7 record for Baltimore's pennant-winning team. But it was the next year that Stone stepped into the spotlight. He led the majors in wins (25–7, 3.23 ERA). He was the owner of a 14-game win streak (May 9 through July 26) and was the starting AL pitcher in the All-Star Game. Stone was named the American League Cy Young Award winner in 1980. However, he developed tendinitis in his throwing arm and retired after the 1981 season.

Stone did not stray far from the game of baseball, as he joined the broadcast booth at ABC and was on one of their regional broadcast teams. Later he teamed with Harry Caray and then Chip Caray at WGN for the Chicago Cubs. He has since moved on to the South Side of the Windy City and currently broadcasts games for the Chicago White Sox.

Duane Kuiper was the regular second baseman for the Indians from mid-1975 to 1981. Defense was his calling card, and he could flash the leather. Going into the ballgame, Kuiper had accumulated 1,382 at-bats without hitting a home run. A few weeks earlier, he had surpassed Milwaukee's Tim Johnson for home run futility. With one out in the bottom of the first, he deposited Stone's 1-0 pitch into the second row behind the right-field fence. His teammates ran out onto the field to greet him at home plate. It was to be his only home run in 3,379 at-bats. The Indians won the game, 9–2.

"Me and Sadaharu Oh," Kuiper quipped, referring to the baseball legend from Japan who hit a record 868 home runs. "Actually, I didn't think of anything rounding the bases. I think I hit a slider. When I got back to the dugout, I tried to think back. Did I touch all the bases? I knew it would happen. Eventually, it has to happen. It was a big thrill. You lose perspective sometimes, it makes for a lot of laughs, and I might like to have kept my homerless streak alive. But a home run has to happen, even by accident."

The game was televised by ABC, and the broadcast was beamed back to Kuiper's hometown in Racine, Wisconsin. Al Michaels called the broadcast that evening. Although Michaels is noted for coining the phrase "Do You Believe in Miracles" with relation to the USA ice hockey team defeating the Russians in 1980, there are some who wonder if this game was the first time that phrase was actually uttered.

Kuiper, like Stone, went into broadcasting after his career, and he teamed with Jon Miller and former pitcher Mike Krukow to call Giants games for decades. On April 25, 2014, San Francisco hosted Cleveland in an interleague matchup. To commemorate Kuiper's feat, the first game in the series was Duane Kuiper Bobblehead Day. Krukow would often make light of Kuiper's lone home run during a broadcast. When a Giants player would hit his first career home run, Krukow would exclaim, "And he has just tied Duane Kuiper on the All-Time home run list."

3. On October 10, 1920, the Cleveland Indians defeated the Brooklyn Robins by a score of 8–1. The ballgame drew a sell-out crowd of 26,884 to Dunn Field. The pitching matchup was a carbon copy of Game Two—Burleigh Grimes got the start for Brooklyn and Jim Bagby for Cleveland. Brooklyn had won Game Two by the score of 3–0 four days earlier at Ebbets Field.

The Indians were responsible for providing three firsts in World Series history. In the bottom of the first inning, Charlie Jamieson led off by hitting a ball to Robins first baseman, Ed Konetchy. But Konetchy could not field the ball cleanly, and Jamieson was given credit for a hit. Bill Wambsganss followed with a clean single to left field. Tris Speaker laid down a bunt toward the mound, and when Grimes fell down trying to hurry his throw, Speaker had a hit. With the bases loaded, Elmer Smith crushed a home run over the right-field wall and the 45-foot screen atop it. It was the first grand slam in World Series history. The Cleveland fans erupted at the historic blast, and the noise did not let up for the remainder of the game.

Cleveland increased its advantage in the fourth inning when first baseman Doc Johnston singled off of Grimes's leg. He went to second on a passed ball charged to Robins catcher Otto Miller. A groundout by Joe Sewell moved Johnston along to third base. With Bagby on deck, Tribe catcher Steve O'Neill was given a free pass with the hope that the Robins could turn two. Bagby upset that strategy with a home run to right center, the first home run by a pitcher in World Series play. Cleveland led, 7–0.

In the fifth inning, the Robins got consecutive singles from Pete Kilduff and Miller. Brooklyn pitcher Clarence Mitchell (who relieved Grimes in the fourth inning) stepped up to the plate and hit a liner to second baseman Wambsganss. Wamby moved to his right, leaped, and snared the liner. The runners were moving, and Wamby stepped on second base, turned, and tagged a shocked Miller barreling toward him for an unassisted triple play. The Robins' catcher was not the only one caught off guard. The whole park fell silent, trying to figure out what had just unfolded on the field. Then cheers erupted through the autumn air. Almost a century later, it remains the only unassisted triple play in a World Series.

4. Miguel Dilone stole 61 bases in 1980 for the fourth-highest total by an Indians player in a season. At the time, Dilone held the single-season record, snapping the previous mark of 52 stolen bases by Ray Chapman in 1917. Kenny Lofton has the highest stolen base total in a season with 75 in 1996, 70 in 1993, 66 in 1992, and 60 in 1994.

Dilone was born on November 1, 1954, in Santiago of the Dominican Republic. He was originally signed by the Pittsburgh Pirates as an amateur free agent on April 20, 1972. He made his major-league debut with the Pirates on September 2, 1974.

In 12 major-league seasons, the much-traveled Dilone played for seven teams: Pittsburgh (1974–77, 1983), Oakland (1978–79), Chicago Cubs (1979), Cleveland (1980–83), Chicago White Sox (1983), Montreal (1984–85), and San Diego (1985).

Dilone was especially fleet of foot and was often used as a pinch-runner early in his career. However, he showed that when given the chance, he could contribute in other ways. Not only did Dilone lead the Tribe in stolen bases in 1980, but he also was the team leader in batting average (.341), hits (180), doubles (30), and triples (9). A switch-hitter, Dilone was adept at the swinging bunt to get many of his hits. He split time with Joe Charboneau in left field, with Charboneau serving as the designated hitter at other times.

Dilone hit .290 in the strike-shortened season of 1981. He led the Tribe in stolen bases with 29 and again in 1982 with

33. But his batting average dropped to .235 in 1982 and .191 in 1983. Not one to walk with much frequency, Dilone's value was diminished since he could not get on base. The addition of Pat Tabler and George Vukovich as well as Bake McBride cut into Dilone's playing time. He was traded to the Chicago White Sox on September 1, 1983 to complete a deal in which Cleveland received pitcher Rich Barnes.

In four years with Cleveland and 340 games, Dilone batted .289 with 128 stolen bases.

5. Jesse Burkett of the Cleveland Spiders led the National League with a .405 batting average in 1895. Burkett, known as "the Crab" for his cranky and unfriendly demeanor, also batted a league-leading .410 in 1896. "Shoeless Joe" Jackson finished second to Detroit's Ty Cobb (.420) in the American League in 1911, batting .408. Jackson batted .395 in 1912 and again finished second to Cobb, who batted .409.

Jesse Burkett was born on December 4, 1868, in Wheeling, West Virginia. Burkett broke into the big leagues with the New York Giants after stops in Worcester and Indianapolis on the minor-league circuit. Although he batted .309 for the Giants, Burkett was a pitcher who did not hurl too well. In 21 appearances (14 starts), he posted a 3–10 record with a 5.57 ERA. When he was not pitching, Burkett played in the outfield. But his range was limited, and he had a weak arm.

New York sold Burkett to Cleveland in February 1891. The notion of being a pitcher for the Spiders was remote, so Burkett was sent to the outfield on a full-time basis. Cleveland player-manager Patsy Tebeau was willing to sacrifice Burkett's defensive deficiencies in light of his productivity at the plate.

From 1894 to 1898, Burkett never batted below .340. In eight years with Cleveland, Burkett hit .355 with 33 home runs and 512 RBIs. For his career, Burkett banged out 2,850 hits and batted .338. Eighty percent of his career hits were singles.

Burkett was elected to the Hall of Fame in 1946. He passed away on May 27, 1953 from heart disease.

Joe Jackson was born on July 16, 1887, in Pickens County, South Carolina. Growing up in a mill town, Jackson worked in the mills and played on various mill teams as a youngster. He was known as an illiterate, who allegedly signed his first baseball contract with an "X."

Jackson got the moniker "Shoeless Joe" when he was in the Carolina Association and he played a game in his stocking feet because his new cleats were not broken in. "I've read and heard every kind of yarn imaginable on how I got the name," said Jackson. "I never played the outfield barefoot, and that was the only day I ever played in my stockinged feet, but it stuck with me."

Jackson was a complete ballplayer who could run, hit, and throw. A bat was made for Jackson out of a four-by-four wood beam that was cut out from a hickory tree. The bat was blackened with tobacco juice, and Jackson named it "Black Betsy."

Philadelphia Athletics owner Connie Mack purchased Joe's contract for $900 from the Class D Greenville Spinners in 1908. But Jackson was homesick and returned to Greenville. He eventually returned to the A's, but the size of Philadelphia was intimidating to him. Jackson admired Mack. According to Jackson, Mack taught him more baseball than any other manager in his career. But he bounced between the Athletics and the minors the next two years. His teammates on the A's ridiculed him unmercifully because of his illiteracy and, in general, his southern ways. Mack decided Jackson would never make it in Philadelphia and dealt him to Cleveland on July 30, 1910.

Jackson was more comfortable in Cleveland, and the Naps had some other players who were from the south, which made Shoeless Joe less conspicuous about his shortcomings. Joe played for the Naps until 1915, when he was traded to the Chicago White Sox. Jackson was in Cleveland for six seasons and 674 games. He is the franchise leader in batting average (.375), fourth in triples (89), second in on-base percentage (.441), and fifth in slugging percentage (.542). He led the AL right fielders in assists in 1912 (24) and 1913 (28).

Due to financial woes, Cleveland owner Charles Somers was forced to trade Jackson to the White Sox for outfielder Bobby "Braggo" Roth, pitchers Larry Chappell and Ed Klepfer, and $31,500. Jackson hit .301 for the White Sox in 1917 as they won their second world championship. He batted .351 two years later, but the White Sox fell to Cincinnati in the World Series. In what later became known as the Black Sox Scandal, eight members of the White Sox were indicted for fixing the 1919 Series. Although they were found innocent in court, they were given a lifetime ban from baseball by Commissioner Kenesaw Mountain Landis.

Much has been made about Jackson leaving the Cook County Courtroom after giving his deposition and a boy asking "Say it ain't so, Joe. Say it ain't so." But it never happened. "When I came out of the building, this deputy asked me where I was going, and I told him to the South Side. . . . There was a big crowd hanging around the front of the building, but nobody else said anything to me. It just didn't happen, that's all. Charley Owens [reporter for the *Chicago Daily News*] just made up a good story and wrote it."

Jackson's last year in the big leagues was 1920. His life-time batting average was .356, ranking third all-time behind Cobb (.366) and Rogers Hornsby (.359).

Jackson died of a heart attack on December 5, 1951.

6. Bobby "Braggo" Roth was the first to accomplish the deed and Tyler Naquin was the second.

Braggo Roth, who hailed from Chicago, signed his first professional contract in 1910 with Green Bay of the Class D Wisconsin-Illinois League. Even though Roth could hit the baseball and was a fast runner, his defense at third base was woeful. When his contract was purchased by Kansas City of the American Association in 1914, manager Bill Armour moved Roth to the outfield. He also received his nickname because, as one writer put it, Roth was "an entertaining talker and more often than not the hero of his stories was himself." He batted .293 for the K.C. Blues with 12 homers in 1914.

Armour recommended Roth to the White Sox, and they signed him that August. He made his major-league debut on September 1 and gave a good account of himself, batting .294 in 34 games. Chicago acquired outfielder Eddie Murphy from Philadelphia in 1915, which cut into Roth's playing time. When the opportunity came for the White Sox to deal for Shoeless Joe Jackson, Roth was deemed expendable and sent to Cleveland.

Cleveland acquired Tris Speaker in 1916, and Roth hit .286 batting behind him. However, he was part of an ugly incident at Sportsman's Park in St. Louis on August 12 when he was the target of taunts from the crowd at an Indians-Browns game. In retaliation, Roth hurled a bottle into the stands and allegedly struck a patron.

He was still in the lineup on August 13 at Dunn Field. In the bottom of the ninth inning with the scored knotted at three, Roth stepped to the plate and sent a Earl Hamilton fastball over the head of center fielder Armando Marsans. Henry Edwards of the *Cleveland Plain Dealer* wrote, "The Cuban is fleet of foot, but even his speed would not allow him to catch up with the ball, which traveled like a bullet and never stopped until it bounded against the scoreboard. Roth was well past second when the Cuban picked it up. He never hesitated in rounding third and dashed home standing up as Marsans' throw to one of his mates who rushed into the field to act as a relay man went astray." The Indians rushed out to celebrate the victory and Roth's heroics. The fans cheered until their voices turned hoarse at the way the sudden and unsuspecting victory had been delivered.

In 1917, Roth added the stolen base to his offensive repertoire, stealing 51 bases, including home plate six times. But the gregarious and colorful Roth often butted heads with Cleveland manager Lee Fohl. In one of the best trades in Indians history, Roth was sent to Philadelphia for outfielder Charlie Jamieson, third baseman Larry Gardner, and pitcher Elmer Myers on March 1, 1919. Gardner and Jamieson were cornerstones of Cleveland's world championship team in 1920.

In four seasons with Cleveland that covered 415 games, Roth batted .286 with 10 home runs, 223 RBIs, and 130 stolen bases. After leaving Cleveland, he split the 1919 season between the Athletics and Red Sox. He spent one year in Washington (1920) and one with the New York Yankees (1921).

Roth passed away on September 11, 1936, when he was a passenger in a car that was struck by an oncoming newspaper truck in Chicago.

Tyler Naquin was the number one pick (15th overall) by the Cleveland Indians out of Texas A&M University in the 2012 amateur draft.

The left-handed hitter ascended through the Cleveland farm system. He hit .313 in 2014 at Double-A Akron. He batted .348 at Akron in 2015 before being promoted to Triple-A Columbus. A shoulder injury to Michael Brantley, coupled with Marlon Byrd and Abraham Almonte serving suspensions for illegal substance use, opened the door for Naquin to break camp with the Indians in 2016.

He batted .296 with 14 home runs and 43 RBIs while starting in center field. Perhaps his biggest moment occurred on August 19 at Progressive Field. Toronto led Cleveland by a 2–1 score when closer Roberto Osuna was summoned into the game to begin the bottom of the ninth.

The right-handed Osuna had 27 saves to his credit. But no closer is infallible. With one out, José Ramírez lifted a home run to right field to knot the game, 2–2. Naquin stepped to the plate and with the crowd on its feet, cheering rabidly, he also lifted a fly ball to right field. "I was just thinking after I hit it, I took a couple of steps out of the box and just pictured it kicking off the wall," said Naquin. "I thought, 'I have a chance to score if it kicks far enough.' And sure enough, it did."

Indeed, it did. Right fielder Michael Saunders drifted back to the wall but could not come up with the baseball. It bounded to right-center field, where center fielder Melvin Upton Jr. gave chase. As Upton retrieved the ball, he slipped and fell and heaved the ball toward the infield from a prone position. By this time, Naquin was heading to third and being waved home. As his teammates hurried from the third-base dugout, they were seemingly running beside Naquin. He dove headfirst across home plate, well ahead of the tag, to secure the 3–2 Indians win. "That was a pretty cool moment," said Naquin. "I almost fell down there for a second. I wanted to just keep running."

Naquin finished third in the American Rookie of the Year Award voting, trailing Detroit's Michael Fulmer and New York's Gary Sanchez.

7. Tony Peña's base hit to center field to lead off the sixth inning was the only hit by the Indians in Game Six of the 1995 World Series.

Tom Glavine struck out eight and walked three in eight innings of work. Mark Wohlers pitched a 1-2-3 ninth inning for the save. It was Glavine's second win as he was voted the Series Most Valuable Player.

Glavine went on to post a career record of 305–203 with a 3.54 ERA. He pitched for 22 years with Atlanta and the New York Mets, leading the league in wins five times. He won two Cy Young Awards (1991 and 1998) and was elected to the Hall of Fame in 2014.

Tony Peña signed with the Indians as a free agent on February 7, 1994 after playing in Pittsburgh (1980–86), St. Louis (1987–89), and Boston (1990–93). He was on Cleveland's roster for three seasons (1994–96), serving mostly as a backup to Sandy Alomar Jr. He is regarded as one of the top defensive catchers in major-league history and is one of only two backstops (Bob Boone is the other) to win a Gold Glove in each league. Peña was an 18-year veteran, having been selected to five All-Star Games.

One of his biggest moments in an Indians uniform came on October 3, 1995, at Jacobs Field. His solo home run off

Boston's Zane Smith in the bottom of the 13th inning gave the Indians a 5–4 victory. The round-tripper gave the Indians a 1–0 advantage in the AL Division Series over the Red Sox, who they eventually swept in three games. Ironically, it was the Indians' first victory in the postseason since 1948, when they defeated another team from Boston, the Braves, for their second and currently last world championship.

8. Woodie Held, Pedro Ramos, Tito Francona, and Larry Brown each hit a solo home run off Angels relief pitcher Paul Foytack in the bottom of the sixth inning.

Foytack retired the first two batters in the frame before the home run parade began. Held, Ramos, and Brown all homered to left field, while Francona's blast sailed over the right-field fence. For Ramos, the starting pitcher for the Indians, it was his second home run of the game. His first one was hit off Angels starter Eli Grba in the third inning. Brown's homer was the first in his career. The Tribe prevailed by a score of 9–5.

The Indians swept the Angels in the two-night double-header. Fred Whitfield homered for the only Indians run in their 1–0 victory in the opener. Whitfield was also part of the home run party in the nightcap, smacking a grand slam off Don Lee in the third inning. For the season, Max Alvis led the team with 22 home runs and 67 RBIs, as Cleveland hit an anemic .239 as a team.

"What else is there to do but laugh?" said Foytack. "I was glad to get out of there alive. It's the first time I ever was cheered by the fans after leaving the mound on being knocked out." Foytack appeared in two games the following year and then his 11-year major-league career was over.

The power surge by the Indians tied the major-league record that was set just two years earlier. The Milwaukee Braves also smacked four consecutive home runs in one inning against the Cincinnati Reds on June 8, 1961. Eddie Mathews, Hank Aaron, Joe Adcock, and Frank Thomas did the honors. Ironically, Adcock was a member of the 1963 Indians, platooning with Whitfield at first base.

9. Joe Gordon, Graig Nettles, Oscar Gamble, and Mel Hall each hit at least 40 home runs for both the Cleveland Indians and New York Yankees.

Joe Gordon—New York Yankees (1938–43, 1946), 153
Cleveland Indians (1947–50), 100
Graig Nettles—Cleveland Indians (1970–72), 71
New York Yankees (1973–83), 250
Oscar Gamble—Cleveland Indians (1973–75), 54
New York Yankees (1976, 1980–84), 87
Mel Hall—Cleveland Indians (1984–88), 49
New York Yankees (1989–92), 63

10. Pitchers Rick Wise and Mike Paxton, infielder Ted Cox, and catcher Bo Díaz were sent to Cleveland to complete the trade.

Of the four, **Rick Wise** was the veteran. He pitched for Philadelphia (1964, 1966–71), St. Louis (1972–73), and Boston (1974–77). The 1971 season was arguably his best in the major leagues, as he posted a 17–14 record with a 2.88 ERA. In addition, Wise pitched a no-hitter for the Phillies on June 23, 1971 and also homered twice as he beat Cincinnati 4–0. Wise hit six home runs in 1971, one of the highest totals for a pitcher in major-league history.

Wise led the Red Sox to a pennant in 1975, as he led the staff with a 19–12 record with a 3.95 ERA. He won a game in both the ALCS and the World Series.

Wise led the American League in losses as he went 9–19 during his first year with Cleveland. He rebounded to have a respectable 15–10 record in 1979. He finished his career with San Diego (1980–82). In his 18-year career, Wise was 188–181 with a 3.69 ERA. He was a pitcher who had excellent control with 1,647 career strikeouts and 804 walks.

Mike Paxton pitched his way to a 10–5 record for Boston in 1977. He also posted a 5–0 record at Triple-A Pawtucket that same year. The right-handed hurler was 12–11 in 1978 and 8–8 in 1979. In early May 1980, Paxton was sent to Triple-A Tacoma, where he posted a 6–10 record. Paxton pitched his final year in professional baseball in 1981, as he pitched for Triple-A Charleston, the Indians' top affiliate. But after going 6–9 in 19 starts, he was released.

Ted Cox batted .334 at Triple-A Pawtucket in 1977, including 14 home runs and 81 RBIs. He was named Topps Minor League Player of the Year in 1977. He was called up to Boston and made his major-league debut on September 18, 1977. It was "Thanks Brooks" Robinson Day in Baltimore, and Cox ruined the festivities by going 4-for-4. He scored three runs and drove in a run as Boston won, 10–4. "Brooks Robinson came over to the clubhouse after the game to congratulate me on my fast start," said Cox. "It was a day of big thrills, but I almost passed out when he shook my hand, wished me luck, and playfully thanked me for 'ruining his big day.'"

The Red Sox returned home to Fenway Park to face the Yankees. Again, Cox was in the lineup, and he hit safely in his first two at-bats. He set a major-league record with the most consecutive hits at the start of a career. Washington's Cecil Travis had the old record of five in 1933.

Unfortunately, the rest of Cox's career in the major leagues did not fare as well. He played for five seasons (1977–81) with Cleveland, Seattle, and Toronto. He batted .245 with 10 home runs and 79 RBIs.

Bo Díaz was also a member of the 1977 Pawtucket team with Paxton and Cox. He batted .263 but was known more for a rifle arm and as a heady defensive presence behind the plate.

In Cleveland, he served as a backup to Gary Alexander in 1978 and 1979 and then Ron Hassey in 1980. Díaz and Hassey split the catching duties in the strike-shortened 1981 season. Díaz, who threw out 14 of 35 would-be base stealers and batted .313, was named as a reserve to the American League All-Star team.

He was part of a three-team trade on December 9, 1981, that sent him to Philadelphia, where he became the starting backstop. Díaz was a member of the pennant-winning Phillies team in 1983. But knee and back injuries curtailed his playing time the next two seasons. Díaz was traded to Cincinnati in 1985 and was a member of the Reds through 1989. For his 13-year career, Díaz batted .255 with 87 home runs and 452 RBIs. He fielded his catching position at a .986 clip.

Díaz passed away on November 23, 1990. While at home in his native Caracas, Venezuela, it was a windy day and the families' reception from their satellite dish was snowy. Díaz climbed the roof in order to make adjustments, but the dish slipped and fell on Díaz. The impact of the satellite dish broke his neck, killing him instantly.

11. Early Wynn was traded to the Chicago White Sox on December 4, 1957, and won the ML Cy Young Award for the White Sox in 1959.

Jim Perry was traded to the Minnesota Twins on May 2, 1963, and won the AL Cy Young Award for the Twins in 1970.

Gaylord Perry was traded to the Texas Rangers on June 13, 1975, and won the NL Cy Young Award for the San Diego Padres in 1978. He became the first pitcher to win the award in both leagues, having won in 1972 while a member of the Indians.

Dennis Eckersley was traded to the Boston Red Sox on March 30, 1978, and won the AL Cy Young Award for the Oakland Athletics in 1992.

John Denny was traded to the Philadelphia Phillies on September 12, 1982, and won the NL Cy Young Award for the Phillies in 1983.

Rick Sutcliffe was traded to the Chicago Cubs on June 13, 1984, and won the NL Cy Young Award for the Cubs in 1984.

Bartolo Colón was traded to the Montreal Expos on June 27, 2002, and won the AL Cy Young Award for the Anaheim Angels in 2005.

12. Dick Donovan was the honored Tribe hurler in 1962.

He went 20–10 for the Tribe with a 3.59 ERA. He tied for the league lead in shutouts with five. He also hit a career-high four home runs that season.

Donovan, who hailed from Boston, started his major-league career in 1950 with the hometown Boston Braves. But Donovan's career really began to blossom in 1955 when he was dealt to the Chicago White Sox. Over six seasons there, he posted a 73–50 record and was a member of their "Go-Go Sox" pennant-winning team in 1959.

When the original Washington Senators moved to Minneapolis for the 1961 season, an expansion team was placed in the nation's capital. The "new" Senators selected Donovan in the expansion draft. Donovan was second on the team with wins with a 10–10 record, and he led the league with a 2.40 ERA. On October 5, 1961, he was traded to Cleveland with catcher-outfielder Gene Green and infielder Jim Mahoney for outfielder Jim Piersall. At the time of the trade, Tribe outfielder Willie Kirkland said, "Donovan alone will help us more than Piersall. Piersall may have been a team player at the start when we were winning. But later, he was out for Piersall. Maybe he was out trying to win the batting championship. He'd get two hits and say, 'The hell with it,' and leave the game or start bunting."

Donovan retired in 1965, as his role in Cleveland was diminished as he grew older and younger arms made their way to the big leagues. For his career, Donovan was 122–99 with a 3.67 ERA. He hit 15 home runs in his career, which ranks him among the all-time leaders among pitchers in major-league history. Donovan turned to a career as a stockbroker in retirement and also owned his own real estate appraisal office.

He passed away on January 6, 1997, as a result of cancer.

13. Bill Melton manned the hot corner for Cleveland on Opening Day, April 7, 1977, at Fenway Park. He went 3-for-5 with two runs scored in Cleveland's 5–4 victory.

The Gulfport, Mississippi, native was signed as an amateur free agent by the Chicago White Sox in 1964. He made his major-league debut in 1968, and for the next eight seasons Melton served as a third baseman-outfielder-designated hitter for the Chisox. Melton had back-to-back years of hitting 33 home runs in 1970 and 1971. Those 33 homers in 1971 led the junior circuit.

Melton was dealt to the California Angels after the 1975 season. He played sparingly for the Angels, hitting six home runs and driving in 42 runs. Melton was not much of a hitter for average, as he batted .208 in 1976. But the Angels loaded up on free agents, signing Bobby Grich, Don Baylor, and Joe Rudi, making Melton expendable.

He was sent to Cleveland for a player to be named later (pitcher Stan Perzanowski) in December 1976. Melton had a productive exhibition season, batting .306 with seven home runs and 23 RBIs, and was voted the Indians' most outstanding player in spring training.

A dislocated right knee forced the Indians to move projected starting left fielder Johnny Grubb to the disabled list. Buddy Bell volunteered to make the move to left field, and manager Frank Robinson acquiesced. Melton was installed as the opening day third baseman. "I thought it was great that Buddy would be willing to do such a thing for the good of the team," said Robinson.

But after Grubb returned, Bell returned to third base. Melton saw intermittent action the remainder of the season. Melton played his last game on August 30, 1977. That was the day after Duane Kuiper hit his lone home run in the major leagues. Melton had not hit a homer all season. As legend has it, after Kuiper made the grand tour around the bases, Melton decided to hang up his spikes. He retired after 10 seasons with 160 home runs, 591 RBIs, and a batting average of .253.

In retirement, Melton worked in manufacturing and real estate. As of 2017, he serves as a studio analyst for White Sox games on Comcast SportsNet Chicago.

14. Napoleon Lajoie holds the Indians' team record for hitting safely in the most consecutive games, with 31 in 1906.

Lajoie began his streak on June 4 against Boston, and it lasted until July 4 against Detroit. Lajoie went 54-for-123 for a .439 batting average and 21 runs scored. He led the American League in hits (214) and doubles (48). Lajoie finished second in the league in batting (.355), RBIs (91), on-base percentage (.392), and slugging (.465).

The Cleveland Naps finished in third place with an 89–64 record, five games behind first-place Chicago.

Sandy Alomar Jr. nearly tied Lajoie in 1997. Alomar put together a 30-game hit streak from May 25 to July 6.

15. Dennis Martínez and Mark Clark shared the team lead in wins with 11 apiece. Charles Nagy and Jack Morris each had 10 victories to their credit.

Dennis Martínez joined the Indians as a free agent on December 2, 1993. Martínez had already enjoyed a successful big-league career when he joined Cleveland. He was signed as an amateur free agent by Baltimore in 1973. He compiled a 208–165 record in 18 years between Baltimore and Montreal. He led the American League in the strike-shortened 1981 season with 14 wins.

In 1983, Martínez posted a 7–16 record with a 5.53 ERA. Martínez was not used in the ALCS or the World Series as Baltimore went on to win a world championship. His terrible year reflected his addiction to alcoholism. He was arrested on a DUI charge in December 1983. Martínez, who at first denied that he had a problem, came to face his demons and got the help he needed.

On June 16, 1986, Martínez was dealt to Montreal in a three-player deal. In 1987 he posted an 11–4, 3.30 ERA season for the Expos.

In 1991, Martínez went 14–11, led the senior circuit with a 2.39 ERA and pitched a perfect game against the Los Angeles Dodgers on July 28 of that season. He was selected to the All-Star Game in three consecutive years (1990–92).

Cleveland was looking to add some veteran leadership to the club as it moved into their brand new stadium in 1994. Eddie Murray, a teammate of Martínez for years in Baltimore, also signed on the dotted line. Jack Morris also joined the fold just before spring training.

Martínez may have pitched one of the more historic games in Cleveland Indians history. On October 17, 1995 at the Kingdome, Martínez outdueled Seattle's Randy Johnson in Game Six of the ALCS. In seven innings, Martínez struck out three, keeping the Mariners scoreless. He left with the slimmest of margins, 1–0. But the Indians scored three in the top of the eighth inning to win, 4–0. The victory sent the Tribe to the World Series for the first time since 1954.

In his three years with the Indians, Martínez was 32–17 with a 3.58 ERA and 239 strikeouts. In his career, Martínez was 245–193 with a 3.70 ERA.

In retirement, Martínez served as a minor-league pitching coach. He also was the bullpen coach for Houston in 2013.

Martínez is active in baseball-related activities in his native Nicaragua. The country has renamed its national stadium, located in Managua, in his honor.

Mark Clark joined the Indians in 1993 when he was acquired with minor-leaguer Juan Andújar for outfielder Mark Whiten on March 31, 1993.

Dennis Martínez gave the Indians instant credibility when he came aboard. In 1995, Martínez won his first nine decisions and sported a 9–0 record and a 2.35 ERA on July 21.
AP Photo/Mark Duncan.

The Bath, Illinois, native was selected by the St. Louis Cardinals in the ninth round of the 1988 amateur draft. Clark toiled in the Cards' farm system for a few years, enjoying his best year in 1989 at Class A Savannah, where he posted a 14–9 record with a 2.44 ERA for the Sally League club and made his major-league debut with the Cardinals late in the 1991 season.

Clark was 7–5 with the Tribe in 1993. He was used as a spot starter and also made a couple of starts for the Indians' Triple-A affiliate in Charlotte. After his 11–3, 3.82 ERA season in 1994, it appeared that Clark would fill out a spot in the Indians' rotation in 1995. But he was jettisoned to Triple-A Buffalo when he began to struggle. By August, he was used as a spot starter again and in relief. Clark was not used in the 1995 postseason.

Clark was traded to the New York Mets at the end of spring training on March 31, 1996. He found the NL to his liking, going 14–11, achieving a 3.43 ERA with 142 strikeouts against 48 walks for the Mets. His wins, ERA, and strikeouts were tops among the Mets' starters.

The Mets dealt him as part of a six-player deal to the Chicago Cubs on August 11, 1997. Clark pitched well on the North Side, going 6–1 with a 2.86 ERA.

Clark pitched until 2010. His lifetime record was 74–71 with a 4.61 ERA. He totaled 728 strikeouts against 367 walks.

16. Adrian "Addie" Joss was the only other pitcher in Cleveland history to throw a perfect game.

On October 2, 1908, Joss out-dueled "Big Ed" Walsh of the Chicago White Stockings by a score of 1–0 and in the process pitched a perfect game. It was a game for the ages, as both Joss and Walsh would both find their way to the Hall of Fame.

Cleveland scored their only run on a passed ball, as Walsh struck out 15 men in eight innings and held the Naps to four hits. It took Joss only 74 pitches to earn the second perfecto in American League history. The first was thrown by Cy Young of the Boston Americans in 1904.

The crowd was estimated at approximately 11,000. After the game, some of the patrons at League Park stormed the field to carry Joss upon their shoulders to the dressing room. But Joss was wise to the act and made his escape. "I am taking no chances," said Joss. "Suppose they had let me drop. The season is not over yet."

Joss was correct, but Cleveland finished in second place, just a half game behind Detroit in 1908.

17. Wes Ferrell pitched the fifth no-hitter in Cleveland history and slugged one of his 38 career home runs in the victory. Ferrell is considered one of the greatest-hitting pitchers of all time. Five times in his career he had multiple home run games. Over a 15-year career, Ferrell owned a .280 batting average.

He was the younger brother of Rick Ferrell. The older Ferrell was a catcher who played 18 years in the American League with Boston, St. Louis, and Washington. Rick Ferrell was elected to the Hall of Fame in 1984.

Wes Ferrell pitched for the Cleveland Indians from 1927 to 1933, compiling a 102–62 record with a 3.67 ERA. From 1929 to 1932, Ferrell posted at least 20 or more wins each season. He registered 516 strikeouts but issued 526 walks.

Cleveland traded Ferrell to Boston on May 25, 1934, and Wes joined his older brother on the Red Sox. Wes Ferrell led the league in wins with 25 in 1935 and won another 20 games in 1936.

Wes Ferrell also played with Washington (1937–38), the New York Yankees (1938–39), Brooklyn (1940), and the Boston Braves (1941). In his career, Ferrell was 193–128 with a 4.04 ERA. He struck out 985 batters but walked 1,040.

After his playing days, Ferrell managed for a few years in the minor leagues. He passed away on December 9, 1976, during kidney surgery.

18. Joe Evans, who played mostly against left-handed pitchers and was used as a pinch-runner, received his medical degree from Washington University in St. Louis while he was still playing baseball. He was a licensed physician and surgeon whose specialty was obstetrics.

The native of Meridian, Mississippi, was a two-sport star at Ole Miss. Despite his rather small stature of 5-foot-9 and 150 pounds, Evans excelled as a quarterback in football and as a third baseman on the baseball team. Evans inadvertently played baseball for a semipro team and was ruled ineligible to participate in collegiate athletics in 1915.

Cleveland signed Evans in 1915, and he spent most of the year with the Cleveland Spiders of the American Association. In 1916, Evans was farmed out to Portland of the Pacific Coast League. Cleveland manager Lee Fohl inserted Evans as his starting third baseman in 1917, but he batted a dismal .190 and committed 27 errors in the field.

Evans was contacted by his draft board for active duty in World War I. But since he was a medical student, he and many other students practicing medicine were allowed to return to their universities to work towards completing their degree. Evans completed his undergrad studies at Mississippi before completing his internship and residency in St. Louis. The caveat was that Evans would have to fulfill both the fall and spring semesters, which meant he would report to the Indians late and leave the team early.

In 1919, the Indians acquired third baseman Larry Gardner and outfielder Charlie Jamieson from the Philadelphia Athletics. Gardner, who had been a teammate of Tris Speaker's in Boston, was a significant upgrade at third. With Evans missing most of the 1919 season while completing his degree, Gardner stepped right in to the lineup.

Speaker took over managing duties from Fohl in 1919. The new skipper shifted Evans to the outfield in 1920, feeling that with Evans's quickness and agility, the transition would be a simple one. Evans platooned with Jamieson and Jack Graney, both left-handed batters, in left field. The platoon worked as Evans batted .349 in the regular season and .308 in the World Series. Evans followed it up by batting .333 in 1921.

After a subpar season in 1922, Evans decided to retire from baseball to get his practice up and running. But he was lured back to baseball and was traded to Washington for the 1923 season. He played two more years in St. Louis with the Browns before retiring for good.

In 11 seasons, Evans batted .259, with three home runs and 210 RBIs. He was in practice for more than thirty years in Gulfport, Mississippi. He passed away on August 9, 1953 after a year-long bout with esophageal cancer.

19. Johnny Allen (1937) and Gaylord Perry (1974) were the two splendid pitchers who set a club record by winning 15 games in a row.

Johnny Allen initially came up with the New York Yankees, going 17–4 in 1932, his rookie year. Allen joined a pitching staff already boasting future Hall of Famer hurlers Red Ruffing and Lefty Gomez. The Yankees swept the Chicago Cubs in the World Series, as Allen started one game and received a no decision.

Allen's issue was not pitching but his poor attitude and frequent temper tantrums, which put a strain on the Yankees. He was wound a bit too tight for most people's liking. In addition, he frequently held out, seeking a better contract. He was dealt to Cleveland on December 11, 1935, for pitchers Steve Sundra and Monte Pearson.

Allen posted a 20–10 record with a 3.44 ERA in 1936. St. Louis Browns manager Rogers Hornsby realized that Allen would lose his focus on the mound if you razzed him. Each team had bench jockeys who had a special talent for heckling the opposition. Word got out, and teams let loose on Allen.

In 1937, Allen won 15 games in a row starting with the first game of the season and had a chance to tie the record of 16 consecutive wins set by Walter Johnson. Allen was also sidelined for a few weeks because of appendicitis. But a 1–0 loss to Detroit on October 3 ended the streak. The Tiger run scored when a ball went past third baseman Odell Hale. The play sent Allen over the deep end, and twice he tried to throttle Hale.

Allen was off to a 12–1 start the following year before suffering a shoulder injury at the All-Star Game, and he was never the same pitcher again. He pitched five years for the Indians, posting a 67–34 record with a 3.65 ERA. He totaled 505 strikeouts and 342 walks. He also pitched for the St. Louis Browns (1941), Brooklyn Dodgers (1941–43), and the New York Giants (1943–44).

Gaylord Perry was an established pitcher for San Francisco before joining the Tribe. He topped 20 wins in 1966 (21), and he led the NL in wins with 23 in 1970. In one of the classic pitching matchups of the 1960s, Perry threw a no-hitter against Bob Gibson and the St. Louis Cardinals on September 17, 1968. Perry struck out nine batters while Gibson whiffed 10.

Gaylord Perry was as good as advertised when he joined the Indians. His WHIP (walks + hits per inning pitched) while in a Tribe uniform was an incredible 1.104. He cheated father time, pitching until he was forty-five years of age and going 314–265, with a 3.11 ERA in 22 seasons.
Courtesy of Cleveland Public Library/Photograph Collection.

Perry was dealt to Cleveland with shortstop Frank Duffy for pitcher Sam McDowell on November 29, 1971. He won his first Cy Young Award with a 24–16 record and a 1.92 ERA in 1972.

Perry lost the season opener in 1974, then his winning streak stretched from April 12 to July 3 and lowered his ERA from 7.11 to 1.31 in that stretch of games. Perry finished the season with a 21–13 record and a 2.51 ERA. His brother Jim also had a fine year, going 17–12 with a 2.96 ERA. The Indians finished the season with 77 wins. The Perry brothers accounted for 49 percent of the team's total wins.

Perry won his second Cy Young Award with San Diego in 1978. In his career, Perry's record was 314–265 with a 3.11 ERA. He totaled 3,534 strikeouts and 1,379 walks. He threw 53 shutouts and 303 complete games.

20. Ray Caldwell was the pitcher who was struck by a bolt of lightning but shook it off and continued to pitch his way to victory.

Caldwell may have been one of the dominant pitchers of the deadball era. But his appetite for alcohol and the nightlife impeded his success. He was known to take unapproved leaves from his teams and report back days later. The right-hander broke into the big leagues in 1910 with the New York Highlanders. His breakout year came in 1914 with New York when his record was 18–9 with a 1.94 ERA. It was reported that at one time the Washington Senators offered Walter Johnson for Caldwell, which is an indication of how dominant a pitcher he might have been had he walked the straight and narrow.

He would often display acts of misbehaving, followed by repentance, then he would pitch brilliantly, and the cycle would begin over again. He wore down his managers, and despite fines and suspensions, Caldwell continued with his "Broadway training," as Yankees manager Frank Chance called it.

Having exacerbated the situation and frustrating most of those around him, the fun-loving Caldwell was traded to Boston before the 1919 season. However, his shenanigans continued, and he was released on August 4. Cleveland manager Tris Speaker signed Caldwell, and the pitcher turned in a 5–1 record with a 1.71 ERA in six starts.

Speaker tried a new tact with Caldwell. His contract read, "After each game he pitches, Ray Caldwell must get drunk. He is not to report to the clubhouse the next day. The second day he is to report to Manager Speaker and run around the ball park as many times as Manager Speaker stipulates. The third day he is to pitch batting practice, and the fourth day he is to pitch in a championship game."

On August 24, in his first start at Cleveland's League Park, Caldwell led the Philadelphia Athletics, 2–1, with two outs in the ninth. Suddenly, bolts of lightning clustered over the ballpark. Sparks danced along the metal railings. Then Caldwell was hit by the lightning and knocked down, unconscious. One account said that the bolt had entered the metal button on the top of his cap and exited the metal spikes of his shoes. He later told the *Cleveland Press*, "It felt just like somebody came up with a board and hit me on top of the head and knocked me down." A few minutes later, he arose and insisted on finishing the game. He quickly retired the final batter, Joe Dugan, to preserve the win. On September 10, Caldwell pitched a no-hitter against the Yankees, a 3–0 victory. Apparently, Speaker's regimen was working.

He posted his only 20-win season in 1920 for the Indians as they won their first world championship. Caldwell, Jim

Bagby, and Stan Coveleski combined to win 75 games. Over a career that spanned twelve years, Caldwell posted a 134–120 record with a 3.22 ERA. He also was handy with a bat, hitting a career .248 with eight home runs and 114 RBIs.

Caldwell passed away on August 17, 1967.

21. Boog Powell was honored as the Comeback Player of the Year in 1975. It was the second time Powell won the award, as he was the recipient in 1966 as well. He batted .297 for the Tribe in 1975. He led the team in home runs (27) and tied George Hendrick for the team lead in RBIs (86).

John Powell, who hails from Lakeland, Florida, got his nickname "Boog" from his father. "In the South, they call little kids who are often getting into mischief 'buggers,' and my dad shortened it to Boog," said Powell. "Hardly anybody ever calls me John. I don't know if I'd even turn around if someone called me that."

Powell was signed as an amateur free agent by Baltimore in 1959. Two years later at Triple-A Rochester, he blasted 32 home runs and drove in 92 runs. He earned a late-season call-up to the Orioles in 1961, but it was 1962 that Powell began his tenure as the Orioles' everyday first baseman.

After a down year in 1965, where he totaled 17 home runs, 72 RBIs, and batted .248, Powell rebounded to double his home runs to 34 with 109 RBIs while batting .287. The Orioles won their first of four pennants and their first World Series in 1966 with Powell as their first baseman.

Powell was named the American League MVP in 1970 after he belted 35 home runs, drove in 115 runs, and batted .297. Baltimore won their second world championship in 1970. Powell slugged two home runs and drove in five runs in the series. Powell ranks third in home runs (303) and fourth in RBIs (1,063) in Orioles history.

A shoulder injury cut into Powell's production in 1973. He was being shopped around the league, but there were no takers. Enos Cabell took his spot at first base in 1974, and at the end of the year, Baltimore acquired hard-hitting Lee May.

Former Orioles teammate Frank Robinson took over as Cleveland's new manager for 1975. When he was asked if he wanted to acquire Powell for catcher Dave Duncan, Robby responded "Yes, yes, yes."

Most of the attention on Opening Day in 1975 was on Robinson, as he made his debut as the first black manager in major league baseball. Robby's first-inning home run off New York's Doc Medich further amped up the crowd. But it was Powell, who was 3-for-3 with a home run, two RBIs, and three runs scored that carried the day.

More injuries curtailed Powell's 1976 season, and he ended his career with the Los Angeles Dodgers in 1977. His lifetime batting average was .266 with 339 home runs and 1,187 RBIs.

22. Brook Jacoby has hit the most doubles in Cleveland Stadium history with 95. He edged out Dale Mitchell who had hit 94 two-baggers. Lou Boudreau and Andre Thornton each had 93.

Jacoby was drafted by the Atlanta Braves in the seventh round of the 1979 amateur draft. He made his ascent through the Braves minor-league system before making his major-league debut in 1981. He spent the entire 1982 season at Triple-A Richmond of the International League. In 1983, he had his most productive year in the minors, belting 25 home runs and driving in 100 runs while batting .315.

On October 21, 1983, Jacoby was traded to Cleveland with outfielder Brett Butler and pitcher Rick Behenna to complete a trade that was made earlier in the season which sent Len Barker to Atlanta.

Jacoby was inserted as the Indians' third baseman in 1984, and he solidified the position for several years. He enjoyed his best year in 1987, when he had career highs in home runs (32), walks (75), and batting average (.300). Jacoby was a two-time All-Star selection, in 1986 and 1990.

When Cleveland acquired Carlos Baerga from San Diego following the 1989 season, Jacoby was moved to first base. On July 26, 1991, Cleveland traded Jacoby to Oakland, but he returned the following year before finishing his career in Japan. In 11 seasons, Jacoby totaled 120 home runs, 204 doubles, 545 RBIs, and batted .270.

After his retirement, Jacoby stayed active in baseball, moving to the coaching side. He served as a hitting instructor in the minor-league organizations of Cincinnati (2000–02) and then Texas (2003–06, 2014). He returned to the Reds as the hitting coach for the parent club (2007–13). He joined the Toronto Blue Jays in the same capacity in 2015.

23. Brett Butler has hit the most triples in Cleveland Stadium history with 28. Dale Mitchell totaled 26.

Butler was drafted in the 23rd round by the Atlanta Braves in 1979. In 1980, Butler stole a combined 80 bases between Class A affiliates Anderson and Durham and batted .330. Over the next two seasons, Butler split his seasons between Triple-A Richmond of the International League and the Braves. In 1983, Butler started in left field and led the National League in triples with 13. He paced the team with 39 stolen bases.

Butler was traded to Cleveland with third baseman Brook Jacoby and pitcher Rick Behenna after the season to complete an August trade involving Len Barker.

Butler was inserted as the Indians' starting center fielder and leadoff hitter. In four seasons in Cleveland, Butler batted .288 with 95 doubles and 45 triples. He ranks eighth in franchise history with 164 stolen bases. Butler has also stolen the most bases (84) in Cleveland Stadium history.

Butler signed with San Francisco after the 1987 season. He led the NL in runs (109) in 1988 and in hits (192) in 1990. Butler saw his only postseason action in 1989 as the Giants won their first pennant since 1962. But the Giants were swept by the Oakland A's in the World Series.

In 1991, Butler returned to his native Los Angeles and signed with the Dodgers. He led the league in runs (112) and in walks (108) in his first season in LA. In May 1996, Butler was diagnosed with cancer in his tonsils. He underwent rigorous treatment and rejoined the club that September. He played one more season before retiring. In a career that spanned 17 years, Butler batted .290 and collected 277 doubles, 131 triples, and 558 stolen bases.

In retirement, Butler coached for and managed various minor-league teams. In 2012, Butler guided the Reno Aces to the Pacific Coast League championship with a 81–63 record. He served as the third-base coach for the Miami Marlins in 2014 and 2015.

24. Sam Rice, Ralph Kiner, Jack Morris, and Dave Winfield were all members of the Cleveland Indians for one season. Hal Newhouser and Frank Robinson, both members of the Hall of Fame, were on the Indians for the final two seasons of their playing careers.

Sam Rice was a member of the Washington Senators for almost his entire career. From 1915 to 1933 Rice batted at least .290 every season, retiring with a lifetime average of .322. In his career, Rice totaled 2,987 hits, 1,514 runs, 498 doubles, 184 triples, 34 home runs, 1,077 RBIs, and 351 stolen bases.

He was a member of three pennant-winning teams in Washington (1924, 1925, and 1933) and one world championship (1924). In 63 at-bats in World Series competition, Rice batted .302. His one year in Cleveland was 1934, when he batted .293 in 97 games. Rice was elected to the Hall of Fame in 1963.

Ralph Kiner was a member of the Pittsburgh Pirates from 1946 to 1953. He was traded during the 1953 season to the Chicago Cubs, where he played until 1954. He was dealt to the Indians following the season. Kiner was never on a team that reached the postseason.

Kiner was a power hitter, leading the National League in home runs each season from 1946 to 1952. In his career, Kiner smacked 369 home runs, drove in 1,015 runs, and batted .279. In his one year in Cleveland in 1955, Kiner hit 18 home runs and batted .243 in 113 games.

Kiner was elected to the NL All-Star team six times. His uniform number 4 has been retired by the Pirates. After his playing days, Kiner spent fifty-three years broadcasting baseball games, mostly for the New York Mets.

He was elected to the Hall of Fame in 1975.

Jack Morris hails from St. Paul Minnesota, and broke in with the Detroit Tigers in 1977. He became a member of the starting rotation in 1979, posting a 17–7 record with a 3.28 ERA. Morris won 20 or more games in three seasons:

1983 (20–13, 3.34 ERA), 1986 (21–8, 3.27 ERA), and 1992 (21–6, 4.04 ERA). Morris led the Tigers staff with 19 wins in 1984 as they won their first world championship since 1968. Morris threw a no-hitter against Chicago on April 7, 1984 at Comiskey Park.

Morris was a member of two other world championship teams: Minnesota in 1991 and Toronto in 1992. Morris was 4–2 with a 2.96 ERA in seven starts in the fall classic. Morris pitched the Twins to the third world championship in franchise history on October 27, 1991. In Game Seven at the Hubert H. Humphrey Metrodome, Morris went 10 innings, scattering seven hits, no runs and striking out eight. It was his second victory in the series and he was voted Most Valuable Player.

Morris signed with the Indians on February 10, 1994. He and Charles Nagy tied for second most wins with 10. For his career, Morris compiled a record of 254–186 with a 3.90 ERA. He totaled 2,478 strikeouts and 1,390 walks.

He was elected to the Baseball Hall of Fame Class of 2018.

Dave Winfield was a two-sport star at the University of Minnesota (basketball and baseball). He was drafted by four professional teams in three different sports. The Atlanta Hawks (NBA) and the Utah Stars (ABA) drafted Winfield in basketball. The San Diego Padres drafted him with the fourth overall pick in baseball. And even though he never played football in high school or college, Winfield was drafted by the Minnesota Vikings in the 17th round of the 1973 college draft.

Winfield chose the Padres and started a 22-year career in major league baseball. Winfield was a member of the Padres (1973–80), New York Yankees (1981–90), California Angels

(1990–91), Toronto Blue Jays (1992), Minnesota Twins (1993–94), and Cleveland Indians (1995). He was elected to 12 All-Star Games and was a member of two pennant winners (1981 and 1992) and one world championship team (1992).

Winfield had a lifetime batting average of .283. He also totaled 3,110 hits, 540 doubles, 465 home runs, and 1,833 RBIs. For all his success, Winfield led the league in only two categories, both in 1979: RBIs (118) and intentional walks (24).

He was sold by Minnesota to Cleveland on August 31, 1994. But the work stoppage that crippled the major leagues was not resolved, and Winfield became a free agent. He signed on again with the Indians on April 5, 1995, after the labor dispute was resolved. Winfield played sparingly for Cleveland. In 46 games, mostly as a designated hitter, Winfield batted .191.

Winfield was elected to the Hall of Fame in 2001.

25. Jay Bell hit the first pitch he saw in the major leagues for a solo home run in third inning. Bell, who was just called up from the Florida Instructional League, homered off of Bert Blyleven, the player he was traded for a year earlier. He became the first Indian to hit a home run in his first major league at-bat since Earl Averill did the deed on April 16, 1929. "I enjoyed it," said Bell, who had borrowed a bat from Cory Snyder. "It was definitely a thrill hitting it against Blyleven. It's so ironic because I was traded for him."

Bell was the first round pick (eighth overall) of the Minnesota Twins in the amateur draft on June 4, 1984. He was traded to Cleveland, along with pitchers Curt Wardle, Rich Yett, and outfielder Jim Weaver for Blyleven on August 1, 1985. His abilities with the lumber were not the issue with Bell, but rather the leather. After his season was complete at Double-A Waterbury of the Eastern League, Bell was sent to the Florida Instructional League. Although he hit .277 and drove in 74 runs at Waterbury, Bell committed 45 errors from his shortstop position. It was an improvement from 1985, when he committed 59 miscues.

Unfortunately for Bell, his initial game that day was his highlight in Cleveland. Over the next two years he shuffled between Cleveland and Triple-A Buffalo of the American Association in 1987 and Class Triple-A Colorado Springs of the Pacific Coast League in 1988. With Julio Franco entrenched at shortstop in 1987, his opportunities to see playing time was diminished. In 1988, Franco moved over to second base and Bell split time at shortstop with Paul Zuvella and Ron Washington.

Bell was dealt to Pittsburgh on March 25, 1989, for shortstop Félix Fermín. Bell found a home in the Steel City, playing shortstop for eight seasons. The Pirates won the NL East Division three years in a row (1990–92), and Bell was a key component. His defense improved as well, winning the NL Gold Glove in 1993.

Bell was dealt to Kansas City in 1997 and had one of his more productive years offensively. He batted .291 and hit 21 home runs and drove in 92 runs.

Bell signed with the expansion Arizona Diamondbacks in 1997. Bell was the starting shortstop in 1998 and then moved to second base (1999–02). He was a member of their 2001 world championship team.

In his 18-year career, Bell hit 394 doubles, 195 home runs, and totaled 860 RBIs. His lifetime batting average was

.265. He was selected to the NL All-Star team twice in his career (1993, 1999).

In retirement, Bell coached on the major-league level with Arizona (2005–06), Pittsburgh (2013), and Cincinnati (2014–15). In 2017, Bell served as the manager of the Tampa Yankees, the high Class A affiliate of the New York Yankees.

4

HALL OF FAME LEVEL

HALL OF FAME LEVEL

(Answers begin on page 151)

1. On August 14, 1958, which Cleveland Indian stole home twice in one game?

2. On May 24, 1993, this Cleveland pitcher made his second career start, beating Texas, 4–1, on a one-hitter. It was the only complete game of his career. Who was he?

3. *The Sporting News* named which Indian player as its AL Rookie of the Year in 1970?

4. On July 27, 1978, this Indians player hit two triples, both coming with the bases loaded. The six RBIs were a career high. Who was this triples machine?

5. The Cleveland Indians have had four players in their career who each had a brother who played for the Cleveland Browns. Who were these sibling duos?

6. The first All-Star Game was played on July 6, 1933, at Comiskey Park in Chicago. Which three players represented the Indians in the original midsummer classic?

7. Between 1971 and 1990, who was the only Cleveland Indian voted by the fans as a starter in the All-Star Game?

8. On December 11, 2001, Cleveland traded Roberto Alomar and two prospects to the New York Mets for which five players?

9. Which slugger, in the process of setting a new Cleveland season home run record of 42 that has since been broken, walked only 36 times to become the only pre-expansion

player ever to hit as many as 40 homers and collect fewer walks than dingers?

10. Which Indians player holds the all-time record for the most double plays by a catcher in a season?

11. On May 26, 1993, at Cleveland Stadium, this Indians player hit a fly ball to right field that bounced off the head of Jose Canseco and then went over the fence for a home run. The Indians edged the Texas Rangers by a score of 7–6. Who was the Indians player who was credited with the round-tripper?

12. On July 5, 1954, this Indian went 3-for-5 at Detroit's Briggs Stadium. All three hits were home runs, and he collected eight RBIs. However, for the year, he totaled five home runs and 18 RBIs. Who was he?

13. What two Indians players share the team record for most RBIs (9) in a single game, accomplished on May 4, 1991 and June 9, 2014?

14. Which Cleveland Indians player smashed a grand slam on the first pitch of his first at-bat in the big leagues on September 2, 2006?

15. On April 12, 1960, Cleveland traded Norm Cash to Detroit for which third baseman, who appeared in only four games for the Tribe in 1960 and never returned to the major leagues?

16. Who were the five Hall of Famers penciled in as the starting center fielder for the Tribe on opening day?

17. On August 11, 1929, Babe Ruth swatted his 500th career home run at League Park. Which Cleveland pitcher gave up the historic blast?

18. As of 2017, there were ten pairs of brothers who each wore a Cleveland uniform. Name them.

19. On September 27, 1984, this player made his only plate appearance as a member of the Cleveland Indians. His lone at bat resulted in a home run that gave the Indians a 4–3 win over Minnesota at Cleveland Stadium. Who was he?

20. On May 3, 1952, the Cleveland Indians fielded the first African American battery. Who were these two pioneers?

21. Which Hall of Fame pitcher served as a bat boy at League Park as a youngster?

22. On August 28, 1926, at Fenway Park, this Cleveland pitcher started and completed both ends of a double-header against Boston. He was credited with a win for both games, and incredibly, he did not record a strikeout in either contest. Who was this Indians pitcher?

23. As of 2017, there have been six pairs of fathers and sons who have worn the Tribe threads. Name them.

24. There have been three players in Indians history that have been credited with making an unassisted triple play. Who are these fielding wizards?

25. What Indians relief pitcher was given the moniker "The Amazing Emu"?

HALL OF FAME LEVEL — ANSWERS

1. Vic Power was the base-stealing thief, swiping home plate in the eighth inning and again in the bottom of the tenth as the Indians edged Detroit, 10–9.

As of 2017, Power was the last player to accomplish that feat.

The Indians trailed Detroit, 7–4, heading into the bottom of the eighth inning. But home runs by Rocky Colavito and Vic Wertz tied the game up. Cleveland went ahead when Power singled home Bobby Avila, moved up to second an error by Tigers catcher Charlie Lau, and then checked into third base on a wild pitch by Bill Fischer. Third-base coach Eddie Stanky told Power to "go if you can get the jump." Go Power did, swiping the plate and turning a three-run deficit into a two-run lead at 9–7.

But the Tigers came back to score two runs in the top of the ninth inning to knot the score. The bags were juiced with Power on base in the bottom of the tenth. Colavito was at the plate with two outs. This time, Stanky instructed Power to "play it safe and see what happens." Power had been bluffing his way down the third-base line, and Tigers pitcher Frank Lary was paying him no attention. "I told Eddie, 'I think I can go,'" Power said in the clubhouse after the game. "He say nothing, so I go." Lary tried to hurry the throw home from his windup, but Power slid home, beating the throw easily. "Those were head plays, not leg plays," said Cleveland skipper Joe Gordon. "Vic isn't particularly fast, but he's got baseball instinct. He bluffed the pitchers beautifully—rushing up the line, pausing long enough to make them relax and then, poof— streaking all the way in."

Those were the only two stolen bases Power had for the Indians that season. In his 12-year career, he was credited with 45 stolen bases.

Yankees scout Tom Greenwade had seen Power play in his native Puerto Rico. Power had moved on to Drummondville in the Quebec Provincial League. After receiving positive reports on his play in Canada, Greenwade signed him.

Power preferred to play first base, but Moose Skowron was blocking his path. The Yankees were being pressured to integrate their club, as the Dodgers and Giants had done years before. But although Power was a top prospect, the Yankees preferred to make Elston Howard their first African American player. Howard was viewed by the New York front office as less controversial, more conservative then Power.

On December 16, 1953, Power was part of an eleven-player deal that sent him to the Philadelphia Athletics. After one season in Philly, Power moved with the rest of the franchise to Kansas City. Known as a splendid defensive player at first base, Power was also a threat at the plate. He topped .300 twice with the Athletics and was a two-time All-Star selection (1955–56). On June 15, 1958, Power was packaged with Woodie Held and sent to Cleveland for Roger Maris, Preston Ward, and Dick Tomanek.

Power was a solid player for the Indians. In his four years with them, he batted .288 and slugged 37 home runs, 115 doubles, and 260 RBIs. It was not only at first base where Power excelled, he showed the ability to play all infield positions when he was called upon.

Power won seven consecutive Gold Glove Awards beginning in 1958 with Cleveland and then Minnesota. He is credited with catching the baseball using just his glove hand. At first it was said that he was "hot-dogging it," but the truth was that he was just that good. His lifetime fielding percentage at first base was .994.

2. Tom Kramer was the pitcher who enjoyed a career-night against Texas in 1993. Kramer struck out eight batters (a career-high) in the game. The one hit he surrendered was a solo home run to left field by Julio Franco in the fourth inning. "His velocity went from 87-89 [mph] to 83 the last two innings," said Tribe skipper Mike Hargrove. "Had the circumstances been any different, we probably would have gone to the bullpen in the seventh inning. But it's not often you get the chance to pitch a one-hitter. And he was still getting people out."

Kramer was selected by Cleveland in the fifth round of the 1987 amateur draft. In 1988 at Class A Waterloo of the Midwest League, Kramer went 14–7 with a 2.54 ERA. He struck out 152 batters while walking only 60 in 198 2/3 innings pitched.

Kramer made his way up the Indians' minor-league chain. He earned a late-season call-up in 1991 after he posted a combined 8–3 record with a 2.18 ERA at Double-A Canton-Akron and Triple-A Colorado Springs. He made his debut on September 12, 1991.

Even though Kramer duplicated his record of 8–3 the following year at Colorado Springs, his ERA jumped to 4.88. The tragic deaths of Steve Olin and Tim Crews, plus the injury to Bob Ojeda due to a boating accident on March 22, 1993, created some vacancies on the Indians' staff. Kramer made the

Tribe's roster and made 39 appearances with 16 starts. His record was 7–3 with a 4.02 ERA.

Cleveland signed veteran pitchers Dennis Martínez and Jack Morris prior to the 1994 season, and Kramer was farmed out to Colorado Springs. His stay was short as he was traded to Cincinnati on May 17, 1994, for minor-league pitcher John Hrusovsky.

Kramer never returned to the major leagues. His last year in professional baseball was in 1998 with Colorado Springs, by then a farm club of the Colorado Rockies.

3. Roy Foster was named Rookie of the Year by *The Sporting News* in 1970. He batted .268 with 23 home runs and 60 RBIs while manning left field for the Indians.

Foster was initially signed by the Pittsburgh Pirates as a free agent in 1963. In five years, Foster never elevated higher than Double-A in the Pirates' minor-league chain. After stagnating a few years, he was dealt to the New York Mets in 1967. At Triple-A Tidewater of the International League, Foster had a breakout year in 1969. He batted .281 and led the team in home runs (24) and RBIs (92).

The Seattle Pilots selected Foster in the Rule 5 draft on December 1, 1969. Bud Selig later purchased the Pilots and relocated them to his hometown of Milwaukee.

But just before the start of the season, Foster and infielder Frank Coggins were dealt to Cleveland for third baseman Max Alvis and outfielder Russ Snyder. Tribe manager Alvin Dark immediately named Foster as the starting left fielder.

Foster, a right-handed batter, excelled against left-handed hurlers, batting .308 while batting .240 against righties. Foster was moved to right field in 1971, and his power numbers dropped to 18 home runs and 45 RBIs while his batting average dropped to .245.

The following year his playing time and his production were on a downward spiral. Foster only appeared in 73 games and hit four homers. He was demoted to the minors in 1973.

Foster never made it back to the major leagues. In 337 games, he slugged 45 home runs, drove in 118 runs, and batted .253.

Foster played in the Mexican League in 1974 and 1975, after which his professional career ended.

Foster passed away on March 21, 2008, after suffering a stroke.

4. In the second game of a doubleheader at Yankee Stadium, Duane Kuiper connected for two bases-loaded triples, tying a major-league record. The feat had been accomplished only twice before: by Elmo Valo of the Philadelphia Athletics on May 1, 1949, and by Billy Bruton of the Milwaukee Braves on August 2, 1959. The six runs driven in were a career high. "That's my most productive game ever," said Kuiper. "I never drove in that many runs in Little League. That's as much power as you'll see out of me."

Kuiper, a native of Racine, Wisconsin, was drafted out of high school and college by five major league clubs before he finally agreed to sign with the Indians in 1972. "They gave me an $8,000 signing bonus, which was about half as much as the Yankees had offered earlier, but my dad and I figured I better take it because the word might get around that I didn't want to play pro baseball," said Kuiper.

Kuiper made his major-league debut on September 9, 1974, a 7–1 victory over Detroit. The winning pitcher was Dick Bosman, who was a second cousin to Kuiper.

Kuiper was sent back to the minors at the beginning of the 1975 season. But an injury to starting second baseman Jack Brohamer gave Kuiper the break he needed. He started the next six seasons.

Kuiper was traded to San Francisco, where he was primarily a backup player from 1981 to 1985.

5. Pat Kelly (Cleveland Indians, 1981) and Leroy Kelly (Cleveland Browns, 1964–73)

Alex Johnson (Cleveland Indians, 1972) and Ron Johnson (Cleveland Browns, 1969)

Karl Pagel (Cleveland Indians, 1981–83) and Mike Pagel (Cleveland Browns, 1986–90)

Wayne Kirby (Cleveland Indians, 1991–96) and Terry Kirby (Cleveland Browns, 1999)

6. Pitchers Wes Ferrell and Oral Hildebrand and outfielder Earl Averill were the players who represented Cleveland in the first All-Star Game. Ferrell and Hildebrand did not participate in the game, while Averill was used as a pinch-hitter and had an RBI single in the sixth inning. The American League won, 4–2.

Oral Hildebrand had the best season of his 10-year career in 1933. He posted a 16–11 record with a 3.76 ERA and led the AL in shutouts with six. It was the only season while he was a member of the Indians where his strikeouts (90) outnumbered his walks (88).

Hildebrand also pitched for the St. Louis Browns (1937–38) and the New York Yankees (1939–40). In his career, Hildebrand was 83–78 with a 4.35 ERA. He struck out 527 batters and walked 623.

Earl Averill is listed among the top ten in various Cleveland batting categories. He is first in runs (1,154), total bases (3,200), and triples (121), third in hits (1,903) and doubles (377), and fourth in home runs (226).

Wes Ferrell, whose brother Rick was a catcher for the Boston Red Sox, was also on the AL roster in 1933. Ferrell's record in 1933 was actually one of the worst in his years as an Indian—11–12 with a 4.21 ERA. He was traded the next season to the Red Sox.

7. Manny Trillo was voted in by the fans as the starting second baseman in 1983. Trillo received 790,343 votes, which topped Jim Gantner of Milwaukee who finished in second place with 685,138 tallies. The All-Star Game was held at Comiskey Park in Chicago on July 6, 1983. Trillo gave a good account of himself as he went 1-for-3 with a run scored. The American League won in a rare laugher, pummeling the Nationals by a score of 13–3. The victory snapped an 11-game losing streak the AL had suffered at the hands of their counterparts in the senior circuit.

Cleveland acquired Trillo from Philadelphia on December 9, 1982. He was one of five players (along with George Vukovich, Julio Franco, Jay Baller, and Jerry Willard) the Phillies swapped for Indians phenom Von Hayes. Trillo was the one "name" player coming to Cleveland. He had been on world championship teams in Oakland and Philadelphia and was selected to multiple All-Star Games. Trillo became the first player in MLB history to be voted by the fans as a starter in one league (Philadelphia, 1982) and then be voted in the other league the following season (Cleveland, 1983). He was the second Indian to be voted in as a starter by the fans (Ray Fosse was the first in 1970 and 1971). Sandy Alomar Jr. was the next Cleveland player to be honored in 1990.

Although Trillo batted .272 for the Indians in 1983, he was traded to Montreal in August. The Expos were in a race with Philadelphia and Pittsburgh to win the NL East. They were looking for some veteran help, but the addition of Trillo wasn't a difference maker, as the Phillies won the division.

8. The Indians traded All-Star second baseman Roberto Alomar, pitcher Mike Bacsik, and former No. 1 pick Danny Peoples to the New York Mets. In return, Cleveland received outfielders Matt Lawton and Alex Escobar, pitchers Billy Traber and Jerrod Riggan, and infielder Earl Snyder.

The deal was not well received in Cleveland. Alomar, who was due to make $8 million in 2002, was coming off a great year for the Tribe. He batted .336 with 34 doubles, 12 triples, 20 home runs, 100 RBIs, and 30 stolen bases. Alomar started his third straight All-Star Game and received the Gold Glove Award as well.

The deal was made in an attempt to infuse the Cleveland minor-league system with some talent that it sorely missed. It was a swap made for the future. It turned out to be a trade that benefited neither team.

Matt Lawton was the only real contributor to come out of the deal. In three seasons with the Indians, Lawton batted .257 with 63 doubles, 50 home runs, and 180 RBIs. Lawton was selected to the AL All-Star team in 2004.

Alex Escobar was billed as a five-tool player (good fielder, good speed, good arm, hits for power, hits for average) and the centerpiece of the deal. Injuries curtailed his progress, as he sat out the entire season in 2002 and 2005. Still, his scouting

Roberto Alomar formed one of the best middle infield combinations in baseball with Omar Vizquel from 1999 to 2001. In three seasons with Cleveland, Alomar hit .323 with 63 home runs, 309 RBIs, and 106 stolen bases.
AP Photo/LM Otero.

profile did not match reality. In two seasons with the Indians, Escobar batted .235 with six home runs and 26 RBIs. His last season in the big leagues was in 2006 with Washington.

Earl Snyder played in 18 games for Cleveland and **Jerrod Riggan** appeared in 31. By 2004, both players had exited the majors. Traber pitched in five different seasons with four teams. His career record was 12–14 with a 5.65 ERA.

As for **Roberto Alomar**, his batting average dropped 70 points the following year in New York. He never recovered his prior ability, and at the end of his career, he came off the bench for the Chicago White Sox and Arizona in 2004. He was one of the great second baseman of all-time, with twelve straight All-Star Game appearances and ten Gold Glove Awards. He was inducted into the Hall of Fame in 2011.

Danny Peoples, a No. 1 draft pick out of the University of Texas in 1996 by Cleveland, never made the major leagues. **Mike Bacsik** pitched for four teams in a five-year major-league career. His claim to fame came on August 7, 2007. While starting for Washington, Bacsik gave up Barry Bonds's 756th career home run, placing the San Francisco slugger at the top of the all-time home run list.

9. Hal Trosky is the Indians slugger who holds this auspicious distinction. In 1936, he clubbed 42 home runs and led the American League in RBIs with 162. The 36 walks were the fewest Trosky had in a full season during his nine years wearing an Indians uniform.

After graduating from high school in 1930, Trosky was pursued by both the Philadelphia Athletics and the St. Louis Cardinals. Both teams were atop of their respective leagues, meeting in the World Series in both 1930 and '31. But it was legendary scout Cy Slapnicka who beat them to the punch, getting Trosky to sign on the dotted line with Cleveland.

Trosky spent the first couple of years of his career in the Indians minor league chain. In 1933, he belted 33 home runs for Toledo of the American Association. Trosky earned a late-season call-up to Cleveland, making his major-league debut on September 11, 1933.

In his rookie season, Trosky clubbed 35 home runs, drove in 142 runs, and batted .330. He set a record for rookies with 374 total bases. If there was a weakness to his game, it was in the field. Trosky, a first baseman, led the AL in errors in 1934 and 1936. But to his credit, Trosky worked hard to improve his footwork, and his errors eventually declined. The extra work paid off as he committed only 10 errors in both 1937 and 1938.

Trosky's name was connected to the "Crybabies" in 1940. Some of the veteran players felt that they had a good chance to win the pennant, but they felt it was an impossible task with Oscar Vitt as the Cleveland manager. The veteran players approached Cleveland owner Alva Bradley to vent their frustrations and urge him to make a change. But Bradley, after some thought, backed his manager. Naturally the players' grievances reached the newspapers, and they were dubbed as the "Crybabies."

Towards the end of his career, Trosky started to deal with constant headaches. Eventually the migraines struck him without notice and left him in much pain. His vision blurred, and it was near impossible to hit the baseball. In February 1942, Trosky said, "For the best interest of the Cleveland club and for myself that I stay out of baseball. I have visited various doctors in the larger cities in the United States, and they have not helped me. If, after resting this year, I find that I am better, perhaps I'll try to be reinstated. If I don't get better, then my major-league career is over."

Trosky spent the 1942 and 1943 seasons on his farm in Iowa. Cleveland sold him to the Chicago White Sox in 1944. Although it was against lesser talent as many of the regular players were serving in World War II, Trosky batted .241 with 10 homers and 70 RBIs for the Sox.

Trosky had a batting average of .313 during his Cleveland career. He ranks fifth in team history in home runs (216), fourth in RBIs (911) and slugging percentage (.551), and sixth in total bases (2,406).

His son, Hal Jr., played one year in the major leagues with the White Sox in 1958.

Trosky passed away on June 18, 1979.

10. Steve O'Neill holds the record for most double plays by a catcher with 36 in 1916.

O'Neill, who hailed from Minooka, Pennsylvania, came from a baseball family. He was one of thirteen children in his family, and brothers Mike, Jim, and Jack all played in the major leagues. Mike (a pitcher) and Jack (a catcher) formed the first brother battery in baseball history when both were members of the St. Louis Cardinals (1902–03).

O'Neill was originally signed by the Philadelphia Athletics off the Class B Elmira roster in 1911. He was assigned to Class B Worcester of the New England League. For a twenty-year old, O'Neill handled the pitching staff and himself like a pro. When Harry Davis, a former first baseman for Connie Mack on the Athletics, took over the managerial job in Cleveland, he asked Mack to let him bring O'Neill with him. Mack agreed and sold O'Neill to the Naps for $3,000.

O'Neill struggled with the bat early in his career. His true value was squatting behind the plate, not standing next to it. When Tris Speaker joined the Indians in 1916, O'Neill asked Spoke for some advice on how to improve his offensive production. "Well," said Speaker, "in the first place go up there figuring you'll get a hit, not that you won't. In the second, try to outthink the pitcher. And in the third, stop swinging at bad pitches."

This was probably easy advice to dispense for Speaker, one of the greatest hitters in major-league history. But there must have been something to it, because O'Neill gradually improved.

In 1920 when the Indians won their first world championship, O'Neill batted .321. He followed it up with a .322 average in 1921.

In his 13 seasons with Cleveland, O'Neill batted .265 with 11 home runs, 220 doubles, and 458 RBIs. Five times he led the AL in double plays and twice in assists. He totaled 198 double plays and 1,698 assists in his career. On January 7, 1924, O'Neill was part of a seven-player deal with the Boston Red Sox. After one year in Boston, O'Neill also played for the New York Yankees (1925) and the St. Louis Browns (1927–28).

O'Neill returned to Cleveland as their field manager from August 1935 through 1937. He also piloted the Detroit Tigers (1943–48), Boston Red Sox (1950–51), and the Philadelphia Phillies (1952–54). He led the Tigers to a world championship in 1945. His managerial record over 14 seasons was 1,040–821 for a .559 winning percentage.

Neill passed away as the result of a heart attack on January 26, 1962.

11. Carlos Martínez led off the fourth inning with a solo home run to right field off Kenny Rogers. As the Rangers' Jose Canseco went back to the track, the ball bounced off his melon for the round-tripper. "I thought it was gone," said Martínez. "Then I thought he was going to catch it. Then I saw it hit him in the head and bounce out. You've got to laugh at something like that. It's kind of funny, but that's the way this game is."

Martínez, a native of Venezuela, was originally signed by the New York Yankees as an amateur free agent on November 17, 1983. After two years in the New York minor-league system, Martínez was included in a six-player swap with the Chicago White Sox on July 30, 1986.

His breakout year came at Double-A Birmingham of the Southern League in 1988. He smacked 14 home runs and drove in 73 runs while batting .277. He was called up to the White Sox late in the season and made his debut on September 2. Martínez hit .300 in 1990 as a reserve first baseman and designated hitter.

He was granted free agency on February 23, 1991, and signed with Cleveland. In parts of the next three seasons with Cleveland, he appeared in 221 games and batted .264. He slugged 15 homers and drove in 96 runs. Martínez was released in April 1994. His last season was with the California Angels in 1995.

Martínez' son, Jose, is an outfielder with the St. Louis Cardinals. Carlos Martínez passed away at age forty on January 24, 2006, after a long battle with cancer.

12. Cleveland first baseman Bill Glynn had the career day at Briggs Stadium. Glynn victimized three different Detroit hurlers in the game. His first round-tripper was a grand slam off Ralph Branca in third inning. He added a two-run shot off Ted Gray in the fifth and a solo homer off Dick Weik in the seventh frame. He added a sacrifice fly to plate a run in the eighth.

Glynn was signed by the Philadelphia Phillies in 1946 and spent one season at Americus of the Class D Georgia-Florida League and a couple of years at Class A Utica of the Eastern League. He was promoted to Triple-A Toronto of the International League in 1949. Although Glynn only batted .263, he showed some power with 23 home runs, and he drove in 98 runs. He earned a call-up to the Phillies, making his debut on September 16.

Philadelphia traded Glynn to Sacramento of the Pacific Coast League for outfielder Gerry Scala after the 1951 season.

The Solons were managed by former Indians second baseman Joe Gordon. Gordon worked with Glynn on his batting technique, and he hit .303 before Gordon recommended Glynn to the Indians, who traded outfielder Dino Restelli for him on July 15, 1952.

Glynn, a left-handed batter, backed up first baseman Luke Easter and pinch-hit in 1952. But in 1953, Easter broke his foot early in the year, and Glynn took over at first base. Although his glove work was solid, his offensive contribution was minimal. Glynn began the 1954 season as the starting first sacker, but the Indians acquired Vic Wertz from the St. Louis Browns in order to add some offensive punch. Glynn was relegated to a late-inning defensive replacement and a pinch-hitter.

The 1954 season was Glynn's last year in major league baseball. He played four more years in the minor leagues, primarily in the Pacific Coast League. He then retired to his native New Jersey.

Glynn passed away on January 15, 2013.

13. Chris James and Lonnie Chisenhall each drove in nine runs in one game. James accomplished the feat on May 4, 1991, in Oakland, and Chisenhall equaled the task on June 9, 2014, in Texas.

Chris James was signed by Philadelphia as a non-drafted free agent on October 30, 1981. He batted .316 with 11 home runs, 73 RBIs, and 23 stolen bases at Triple-A Portland of the Pacific Coast League in 1985. James was now considered the Phillies' No. 1 prospect. When outfielder Garry Maddox went on the disabled list with back trouble in 1986, James was called up to the varsity. He made his major-league debut on April 23 in Montreal.

James bounced between the Phillies and Triple-A the next two seasons. He finally broke into the starting lineup in 1988 as the everyday right fielder. James batted .242, but he led the Phillies in home runs with 19, and he was second in RBIs with 66. As a team, Philadelphia finished in last place with a 65–96 record.

James, who also played third base, was christened as the replacement to Mike Schmidt, who announced his retirement early in the 1989 season. But James could not get his bat going, and while he was in a 0-for-31 slump, James was dealt to San Diego for John Kruk and Randy Ready on June 2.

The stay in southern California was short as James was packaged with Sandy Alomar Jr. and Carlos Baerga and sent to Cleveland for Joe Carter on December 6, 1989.

Primarily used as a spare outfielder and a designated hitter, James was a solid veteran off the bench. On May 4, 1991, at the Oakland-Alameda County Coliseum, James went 4-for-5 with nine RBIs and three runs scored. James, who started the game at first base, hit two three-run home runs off Athletics starter Kirk Dressendorfer. The first came in the first inning, and the second blast came in the second frame. The Tribe drubbed the Athletics, 20–6.

James was granted his release at the end of the season. He made many stops for the remainder of his career, including San Francisco (1992), Houston (1993), Texas (1993–94), Kansas City, and Boston (1995).

In a major-league career that covered 10 seasons, James batted .261 with 90 home runs, 145 doubles, and 386 RBIs.

Lonnie Chisenhall was Cleveland's number one pick, and 29th overall, in the 2008 amateur draft. He ascended through the Indians' minor-league chain. Originally a third baseman, Chisenhall split his time from 2011 to 2013 between Cleveland and Triple-A Columbus of the International League. He made his major-league debut on June 27, 2011.

Chisenhall was the Indians' regular third baseman in 2014. He had a solid season at the plate, batting .280 with 13 home runs and 59 RBIs. On June 9 at Globe Life Park, Chisenhall went 5-for-5 with nine RBIs and three runs. He smacked three home runs in the game. In the second inning, he took Rangers starter Nick Martinez deep for a two-run blast. His next two home runs came off reliever Scott Baker. One was a two-run homer in the fourth inning, and the other was a three-run shot in the eighth inning. He knocked in another run with a double in the sixth. Cleveland trounced the Rangers, 17–7.

Lonnie Chisenhall made a smooth transition from third base to right field. Despite battling through an injury-plagued season in 2017, Chisenhall still hit .288 with 12 home runs and 53 RBIs in 82 games.
AP Photo/LM Otero.

Chisenhall was moved to right field in 2015. On October 7, 2016, Chisenhall's three-run home run in Game Two of the ALDS against Boston carried the Indians to a 6–0 victory.

14. Kevin Kouzmanoff smacked a high fastball for a grand slam at Ameriquest Field in Arlington, Texas.

The historic blast off Rangers rookie pitcher Edinson Vólquez traveled 417 feet to center field and came with two out in the top of the first inning. He was the first player in the American League to accomplish the feat. Two players had accomplished the same feat in the NL: Florida's Jeremy Hermida did it on August 31, 2005, and Bill Duggleby of Philadelphia Phillies did it on April 21, 1898. Kouzmanoff was the first, however, to hit a slam on the first pitch. "I heard I set a record," Kouzmanoff said. "That's pretty cool."

Kouzmanoff was playing at Triple-A Buffalo when he got the call to replace Travis Hafner, who was sidelined with a bruised right hand. Cleveland went on to win the game, 6–5.

Kouzmanoff was selected by Cleveland in the sixth round of the amateur draft in 2003. In 2006, he started the year at Double-A Akron before being promoted to Buffalo. In 94 games between the two clubs, Kouzmanoff slugged 22 home runs, 28 doubles, and drove in 75 runs. He batted .379 with a slugging percentage of .656.

However, Kouzmanoff's time in Cleveland was short-lived. He was dealt with pitcher Andrew Brown to the San Diego Padres for second baseman Josh Barfield on November 8, 2006.

He was the starting third baseman for San Diego (2007–09) and totaled 59 home runs, 246 RBIs, and batted .263. He led the league with a .990 fielding average in 2009. That mark set a record in the National League, as he committed only three errors in 311 chances.

Kouzmanoff was part of a four-player trade to Oakland on January 16, 2010. He started one year for the Athletics but was then traded to the Colorado Rockies during the 2011 season.

He last played in the major leagues in 2014 with Texas after returning to the minor leagues for a couple of years. In his career, he hit 87 home runs, collected 371 RBIs, and batted .257. His career fielding percentage at the hot corner was .961.

15. Steve Demeter was the player Cleveland obtained for Cash. It may be considered the worst trade in franchise history. Cleveland had acquired Cash as part of a seven-player deal with the Chicago White Sox on December 6, 1959.

Cash never suited up for Cleveland, as he was dealt to the Tigers before the season began. The deal for Demeter does not get mentioned much, as it was made five days before Cleveland made another deal with the Tigers: Rocky Colavito for Harvey Kuenn.

Cash went on to have a tremendous career with Detroit. In 15 seasons, he slugged 373 home runs and collected 1,088 RBIs while batting .272. Cash ranks second all-time in Detroit franchise history in home runs.

Demeter, a third baseman, appeared in only four games and had five at-bats in 1960. He was sent to the minors and never returned to the big leagues. Demeter played mostly with Triple-A clubs Toronto and Rochester of the International League.

He was elected to the International League Hall of Fame in 2009. Demeter played 11 seasons, totaling 159 home runs and 778 RBIs. He was a three-time postseason All-Star.

After his playing days, Demeter spent 30 years in the Pittsburgh Pirates organization, serving mostly as a scout and a minor league coach/manager.

On February 3, 2013, Demeter passed away as a result of heart disease. His grandson, Derek Dietrich, has been a member of the Miami Marlins since 2013.

16. Elmer Flick, Tris Speaker, Earl Averill, Bob Lemon, and Larry Doby are the five Hall of Famers to roam center field for the Indians on opening day.

With the exception of Lemon, the other four players were elected based on their work in the field and at bat. Doby made the transition from playing second base in the Negro Leagues to center field in the majors. Center field was the normal position for Flick, Averill, and Speaker.

Lemon was the starting center fielder on April 16, 1946, at Comiskey Park. Bob Feller threw a three-hitter, defeating the White Sox 1–0. Lemon was 0-for-3 at the plate. He made four putouts and one assist.

17. Willis Hudlin gave up home run number 500 to Ruth in the second inning. It was the Babe's 30th dinger of the season. The baseball soared over the right field wall and the extended screen and landed onto Lexington Avenue. The *New York Times* reported that the ball "left home plate much higher and ten times faster than it arrived." According to the *Plain Dealer*'s sportswriter Gordon Cobbledick, Ruth knew he would smack the ball out of the park that day and said as much to Clay Folger, head of security at League Park. "Listen," said Ruth, "I'm going to hit No. 500 today, and I tell you what I wish you'd do. I wish you'd find the kid who gets the ball and bring him to me. I'd kinda like to save that one."

Hudlin, who also gave up a solo home run to Lou Gehrig in the fourth inning, rebounded to pitch a complete-game victory, as the Indians won, 6–5.

A native of Wagoner, Oklahoma, Hudlin was a star athlete in high school. He excelled in baseball, basketball, and football, but it was a baseball pitcher he aspired to be one day. He signed with the Class A Waco Cubs of the Texas League in 1926. After hurling consecutive shutouts, Fort Worth manager Jake Atz claimed that Hudlin was the best young prospect he had ever seen. Cleveland scout Cy Slapnicka outbid Cincinnati and the New York Yankees for his services, shelling out $25,000 and two players. Hudlin went 16–11 with a 4.29 ERA in 1926 at Waco before joining Cleveland in August.

Manager Tris Speaker was impressed with his new hurler. "The first time I hit against Hudlin in batting practice, I realized Cleveland had picked a jewel," said Speaker. "He had me, as well as the other regulars on the club, waving a bat at his fastball."

He was a regular in Cleveland's starting rotation for the next 13 seasons. He was not a pitcher who would strike out a lot of batters. His career high was 83 strikeouts in 1931. He had control problems and usually walked more batters then he whiffed over the course of a season. Yet he usually posted double-digit wins. Perhaps his best game came on August 24, 1935, at League Park, a complete-game, 15-inning shutout of the Philadelphia Athletics. He struck out six and walked one in the 2–0 win. Earl Averill's two-run homer in the bottom of the 15th inning ended the marathon.

Over the course of 15 seasons wearing a Cleveland uniform, Hudlin was 157–151 with a 4.34 ERA. He also totaled 31 saves and struck out 662 batters, while walking 832. He ranks seventh in wins in franchise history.

Hudlin was released by the Indians on May 13, 1940. He pitched for three other teams that season: Washington, the New York Giants, and the St. Louis Browns.

He returned to the minor leagues, pitching for the Class A Little Rock Travelers of the Southern Association (1941–46) and the Class B Jackson Senators of the Southeastern League (1947–48). He appeared in one game for the Browns in 1944.

Hudlin also managed in the minors with Jackson (1947–50), Class C Greenville of the Cotton States League (1954–55), and Class A Augusta (1956). From 1957 to 1959, Hudlin was the pitching coach for the Detroit Tigers. After he left the playing field, Hudlin was a scout for the Yankees from 1960 to 1974.

Hudlin passed away on August 5, 2002, in Little Rock, Arkansas.

18. The ten pairs of brothers who each wore a Cleveland uniform were:

Sandy Alomar Jr. (1990–2000) and Roberto Alomar (1999–2001)

Dick Brown (1957–59) and Larry Brown (1963–71)

Jolbert Cabrera (1998–2002) and Orlando Cabrera (2011)

Joey Cora (1998) and Alex Cora (2005)

Vean Gregg (1911–14) and Dave Gregg (1913)

Bill Hinchman (1907–09) and Harry Hinchman (1907)

Jim Perry (1959–63, 1974–75) and Gaylord Perry (1972–75)

Herbert Perry (1994–96) and Chan Perry (2000)

Joe Sewell (1920–30) and Luke Sewell (1921–1932, 1939)

Jesse Stovall (1903) and George Stovall (1904–11)

19. Jamie Quirk hit a home run in his only at-bat in a Cleveland uniform.

Quirk was in his tenth season in the majors in 1984, but he was released by St. Louis during spring training and was offered a job as their bullpen coach. But when the White Sox' Carlton Fisk was injured, Quirk was signed by Chicago on May 23. When Fisk returned to the lineup, Quirk was sent to Triple-A Denver. He finished out the season there and returned to his home in Kansas City.

When Cleveland's regular catcher, Chris Bando, bruised his leg, they signed Quirk as a precaution on September 24. "I'd like to do as good a job as possible over the last six games and hopefully earn an invitation to camp in the spring," said Quirk. "I was at home in Kansas City when I got the call Sunday. I was just thrilled to death. I don't care what the name of the city is, I'm back in the major leagues."

Cleveland's last series of the season was at home against the Minnesota Twins, who were in a fight for first place in the American League West title with Kansas City. The Twins were rolling steadily along, leading 3–0 until the bottom of the eighth inning, when Cleveland scored three runs. During the Tribe rally, starting catcher Jerry Willard was lifted for a pinch-runner, and Quirk replaced him in the lineup.

Twins reliever Ron Davis started the ninth inning by striking out George Vukovich and Pat Tabler. Quirk stepped in the batter's box. He hit a 1-1 fastball just inside the right-field foul pole for the winning hit. "He threw me a curve before that," said Quirk. "But I am not going to swing at a curve with less than two strikes.

"I was talking to some of the Royals at Paul Splittorff's retirement party, and they knew we finished up against Minnesota," said Quirk. "They said, 'Hey, do what you can to help us.' I don't know what more I can do than this." Indeed, the Royals went on the win the AL West.

Quirk went on to play eight more seasons. In all, he played 18 years in the majors. In a career where he was mostly a backup catcher, Quirk played in 984 games. He hit 43 home runs with 247 RBIs. His lifetime batting average was .240. After his playing days, Quirk spent 19 years as a major-league coach, his last year being 2013 with the Chicago Cubs. He is currently a minor-league manager, most recently with the Wilmington Blue Rocks, the Kansas City Royals' affiliate in the Class A Carolina League.

20. Pitcher Sam "Toothpick" Jones and catcher Quincy Trouppe became Cleveland's first African American battery in their 7–6 loss to the Washington Senators. Trouppe relieved starting catcher Birdie Tebbetts in the seventh inning. Jones relieved Lou Brissie in the same inning.

Sam Jones, who hailed from Stewartsville, Ohio, played both football and basketball as a youngster. It was not until he joined the United States Army in 1943 that he began to play baseball. He was stationed at the Orlando Army Air Base near the Pinecastle Army Airfield. The base was segregated so Jones served as a catcher and first base on the smaller teams around the base. It was in the service that Jones developed the habit of chewing on a toothpick. "They've got to be flat," said Jones.

"They're the only kind to chew. The round ones are too hard. The flavored ones don't taste good. I've tried peppermint, cinnamon, even strawberry—they can't touch a plain old flat one."

After the service, Jones joined the Cleveland Buckeyes, where Quincy Trouppe was the manager. The Buckeyes were the Negro League champions in 1947. Sam Jethroe, Al Smith, and Chet Brewer were also on the Buckeyes roster. The Buckeyes lost to the New York Cubans in five games of the Negro World Series.

Two years later, Jones, who was dismissed by Indians scouts earlier, pitched for Hank Greenberg. The former Detroit slugger was the Indians' farm director and later their general manager. "I saw this big fellow pitch, and it was hard for me to believe what I saw," said Greenberg. "Here was a fellow, twenty-three years old, who had never played organized ball and he could do things with a baseball that many of our veterans couldn't do. He had an overhand curve and a sidearm curve. And speed! What speed! How our scout was able to make such a completely incorrect report I'll never understand."

Jones was signed by the Indians in 1950 and posted a 17–8 record at Class A Wilkes-Barre of the Eastern League. He made his major-league debut with the Indians on September 22, 1951.

Jones pitched minimally for Cleveland in 1951 and 1952. He spent a couple of seasons with Triple-A Indianapolis of the International League. He was traded to the Chicago Cubs in a September 30, 1954, deal which brought Ralph Kiner to Cleveland.

Jones pitched a no-hitter against the Pittsburgh Pirates in 1955 and had the distinction of leading the National League in losses (20), strikeouts (198), and walks (185) that season. He would repeat leading the NL in both strikeouts and walks in 1956 and 1958.

Perhaps his best season was in 1959 with San Francisco. Toothpick led the league in wins (21–15) and ERA (2.83) and totaled 209 strikeouts. In his 12-year major-league career, Jones was 102–101 with a 3.59 ERA. He totaled 1,376 strike-outs and 822 walks. He was named NL Pitcher of the Year by *The Sporting News* in 1959.

Trouppe, who hailed from Dublin, Georgia, signed his first professional contract with the St. Louis Stars of the Negro National League. According to Seamheads.com, Trouppe had a .282 batting average. He played with Detroit, Homestead, Chicago, New York, Cleveland, and Kansas City, but statistics are incomplete. He also played in the Mexican League.

He was playing winter ball in Venezuela when Green-berg reached out to Trouppe about joining the Indians. But Trouppe was thirty-nine years old and played in only six games with Cleveland in 1952, as he was stuck behind Birdie Tebbetts and Jim Hegan at catcher. After his playing career, he was a member of the scouting department of the St. Louis Cardinals.

Trouppe passed away as the result of Alzheimer's disease on August 10, 1993.

21. Richard "Rube" Marquard was the young lad who tended to the players' bats in the early 1900s.

Marquard, whose father was the chief engineer for the City of Cleveland, went against his father's demands of a for-mal education. Instead, he chased his dream of being a baseball pitcher.

Marquard holds the major-league record for most con-secutive wins in a season with 19. While pitching for the New

York Giants, Marquard posted a 19–0 record with a 1.63 ERA from April 11 through July 3, 1912. He led the National League with a 26–11 record in 1912.

Marquard, a left-handed pitcher, got his nickname because his delivery resembled that of Rube Waddell, a left-handed pitcher for the Philadelphia Athletics.

Rube played for the Giants, Robins, Reds, and Braves over an 18-year career. His lifetime record was 201–177 with a 3.08 ERA. An excellent control pitcher, Marquard totaled 1,593 strikeouts and 858 walks.

Marquard was a member of five pennant-winning clubs. He was 2–5 with a 3.07 ERA in World Series play. In 1920, Marquard was a member of the Brooklyn Robins as they faced his hometown Cleveland club in the World Series. Marquard was arrested before Game Four on charges of scalping tickets. He was seized in a hotel lobby when he offered to sell eight box-seat tickets that cost $52.80 to a Cleveland police detective for $350. He was eventually fined one dollar in Common Pleas Court.

He was inducted into the Hall of Fame on August 9, 1971.

Marquard died on June 1, 1980, after a two-year battle with cancer.

22. Dutch Levsen threw two complete game victories in the doubleheader at Fenway Park. Cleveland won the opener, 6–1, and also the nightcap by the score of 5–1. Levsen scattered four hits in each game.

Levsen pitched six seasons (1923–28) in the major leagues, all with Cleveland. His first three years he shuttled between the Indians and the minor leagues. The 1926 season was the lone

one in his career where he spent the entire season in the starting rotation. He went 16–13 with a 3.41 ERA. He issued 85 free passes, while striking out 53 batters in 237 1/3 innings.

Levsen's major-league career numbers were 21–26 with a 4.17 ERA. He passed away on March 12, 1972.

23. The six father-son cominations to play for the Indians were:
Earl Averill (1929–39) and Earl Averill Jr. (1956, 1958)
Jim Bagby Sr. (1916–22) and Jim Bagby Jr. (1941–45)
Buddy Bell (1972–78) and David Bell (1995, 1998)
Camilo Carreon (1965) and Mark Carreon (1996)
Dave Duncan (1973–74) and Shelley Duncan (2010–12)
Tito Francona (1959–64) and Terry Francona (1988)

24. The following players, and the dates that the unassisted play was made:
Neil Ball, July 19, 1909
Bill Wambsganss, October 10, 1920
Asdrúbal Cabrera, May 12, 2008
Neil Ball, a shortstop for the Cleveland Naps in 1909, made the play at League Park. Boston's Heinie Wagner and Jake Stahl singled to lead off the second inning. Andy McConnell stepped in the box. On the hill was Cy Young. McConnell lined a 3-2 pitch to short. With the full count on the batter, the hit-and-run play was on. Ball leapt in the air, snagged the liner, and stepped on second base to double off Wagner. He tagged Stahl for the third out. It was the first unassisted triple play in major-league history. "I thought I could spear it and had visions of a double play," said Ball. "I reached into the air and came down with the ball. By this time, Wagner was on third and Stahl was only a few feet from second. I ran over and touched second for

the second out. Stahl was slowing up and reversed his tracks toward first, but I overtook him and tagged him out to complete the triple play.

"I didn't think there was a chance of getting it, but I was on the move toward second, and I gave it a try anyhow. It was dead over the bag by then, so I jumped and the darned thing hit my glove and stuck. The rest was easy. Wagner was way around third base somewhere and when I came down on the bag he was out. I just stood there with my hands out and Stahl ran into them. He was halfway down when the ball was hit and couldn't stop. That's all there was to it. I can still remember how surprised I was when the ball hit in my glove."

Often, when a player makes an exceptional play in the field, he leads off the following inning. Ball led off the bottom of the frame for the Naps and hit his only home run of the season off Boston pitcher Charlie Chech.

Ball had a seven-year career that included stops with the New York Highlanders (1907–09), Cleveland Naps (1909–12), and the Boston Red Sox (1912–13). He was a member of the Boston Red Sox world championship team in 1912.

In 502 games, Ball batted .250 with four home runs and 151 RBIs.

Bill Wambsganss made his play in Game Five of the 1920 World Series at League Park. The Brooklyn Robins had runners on first and second with none out in the fifth inning. Robins pitcher Clarence Mitchell stepped into the box. The result was almost a carbon copy of the play Ball made eleven years earlier. But Wamby was stationed at second base when he snared Mitchell's line drive, stepped on second and tagged Otto Miller for the third out. It remains the only unassisted triple play in World Series history.

Wambsganss, a Cleveland native, was one of the best fielders in the Deadball Era. Primarily a second baseman who occasionally could play some at shortstop, Wamby was not a power hitter or a hitter for average like his predecessor Nap Lajoie.

Bill Wambsganss was a sound all-around player for Cleveland. Nicknamed "Wamby," he was versatile and durable. He led the league in innings played by a second baseman in 1919 and 1920. Wamby (left) is shown here with Yankees manager Miller Huggins (center) and Tris Speaker.
Courtesy of Cleveland Public Library/Photograph Collection.

He led the AL twice in sacrifice hits and often made the key offensive play when it was needed.

In his 10-year career with Cleveland, Wamby batted .258 with 1,083 hits, six home runs, and 429 RBIs. He also played with the Boston Red Sox (1924–25) and the Philadelphia Athletics (1926). His career fielding percentage in 1,205 games at second base was .958.

Asdrúbal Cabrera turned the trick against the Toronto Blue Jays at Progressive Field. Kevin Mench and Marco Scutaro led off the top of the fifth inning with consecutive singles. With both runners moving on the pitch, Lyle Overbay hit a low line drive to Cabrera at second base. Cabrera stabbed it and stepped on second base for the second out and tagged Scutaro for the third.

Cabrera originally signed with the Seattle Mariners as an amateur free agent on August 26, 2002. He was traded to Cleveland for Eduardo Pérez on June 30, 2006.

Cabrera came into the limelight in 2007. He began the year at Double-A Akron and batted .310 for the Aeros. He was promoted to Triple-A Buffalo, and in nine games there, he batted .316. The Cleveland front office was not happy with the play of Josh Barfield at second base and looked for an infusion of offense. Cabrera was brought up to Cleveland, making his major-league debut on August 8.

Cabrera batted .283 his rookie year and was an important element as the Indians won their first AL Central Division in six years. He shifted to shortstop after the Indians moved Jhonny Peralta to third base in 2009.

His best season was in 2011 when he clubbed 25 home runs and collected 92 RBIs while batting .273. He was a two-time All-Star with the Indians in 2011 and 2012.

In his eight years and 914 games with Cleveland, Cabrera batted .270 with 82 home runs and 430 RBIs. In 2017, he completed his second season with the New York Mets.

25. Jim Kern was given the nickname "The Emu."

"The emu stuff began in 1976," said Kern, "when Fritz Peterson and Pat Dobson were with us. One Sunday morning in the clubhouse they were working on a crossword puzzle, and I was doing my usual crazy stuff, running around crowing and flapping my arms. One of the clues in the crossword puzzle was the name of the world's largest non-flying bird." The answer of course was "emu," and Kern extended the moniker to the "Amazing Emu."

Kern was signed by Cleveland as a non-drafted free agent on September 4, 1967. After rookie ball, Kern enlisted in the United States Marine Corps where he served one year active duty and five years in the reserves. He returned to the minor leagues, and on May 29, 1971, Kern threw a no-hitter while pitching for Class A Reno against San Jose. The game was the opener of a doubleheader, thus was a seven inning contest.

Kern was named the American Association Pitcher of the Year in 1974 when he posted a 17–7 record with a 2.52 ERA for Triple-A Oklahoma City. He earned a call-up to Cleveland and made his major-league debut against Baltimore on September 6, 1974. He went the distance in losing, 1–0, to the Orioles and Mike Cuellar.

New Indians manager Frank Robinson put Kern in the bullpen at the start of the 1975 season. But when Jim Perry faltered with a 1–5 record, Kern took his place in the rotation. "Jim has done an outstanding job for us," said Robby. "He's so much more valuable working out of the bullpen, though

I know he can start if necessary. When I came to the Indians, everybody told me about Kern's potential, but it seems that's all they were able to talk about—his potential.

"The line on Jim always was the same—if he can throw strikes, there's no doubt he can win in the big leagues. But the trouble always was that part about throwing strikes."

Paired with Dave LaRoche, the Indians had a solid righty-lefty relief tandem. But when LaRoche was dealt to the Angels in 1977, Kern became the main man in the bullpen.

Kern established himself as a top reliever in 1976. He posted a 10–7 record with a 2.37 ERA and 15 saves. In 117 2/3 innings pitched, Kern struck out 111 batters while walking only 50. His control was vastly improved from his minor-league days. He was selected to the first of three consecutive All-Star teams in 1977. He was 3–6 with a 2.97 ERA at the break and third in the American League with 12 saves.

Kern was vocal about the losing culture in Cleveland, and on October 3, 1978, he and infielder Larvell Blanks were dealt to Texas for outfielder Bobby Bonds and pitcher Len Barker. He posted 29 saves for the Rangers with 1.57 ERA in 1979. His record was 13–5 as he was the recipient of the Rolaids Relief Award as the league's top reliever.

That was the high-water mark for Kern. A hard-thrower, Kern battled arm troubles for much of his career after 1979. He played for a multitude of teams after the Rangers including Cincinnati (1982), Chicago White Sox (1982–83), Philadelphia (1984), Milwaukee (1984–85), and Cleveland (1986). He never appeared in more than 16 games in a season during these years.

In a total of 416 games, Kern had a record of 53–57 and an ERA of 3.32. He totaled 651 strikeouts, 444 walks, and 88 saves. Kern retired to Arlington, Texas, after his playing career. In 1987, he began the Emu Outfitting Company. "I had been a hunter and fisherman all my life, so it was a natural extension for me," said Kern. "We run hunting and fishing trips to Alaska, Zambia, South Africa, Uruguay, Argentina . . . actually almost any place you might want to go to hunt and fish." He also stayed close to baseball. Kern worked for twelve years as a color commentator on college baseball games for FOX Sports Southwest.

Bibliography

Books

Alexander, Charles. *Spoke: A Biography of Tris Speaker*. Southern Methodist University Press, 2007

Dolgan, Bob. *Heroes, Scamps and Good Guys*. Gray & Company, 2003

Fleitz, David. *Shoeless: The Life and Times of Joe Jackson*. McFarland & Co., 2001

_____. *Napoleon Lajoie: King of Ballplayers*. McFarland & Co., 2013

Longert, Scott. *No Money, No Beer, No Pennants: The Cleveland Indians and Baseball in the Great Depression*. Ohio University Press, 2016

_____. *The Best They Could Be*. Potomac Books, 2013

Macht, Norman. *Connie Mack, The Grand Old Man Of Baseball: In His Final Years, 1932–1956*. University of Nebraska Press, 2015

Pluto, Terry. *The Curse of Rocky Colavito*. Simon and Schuster, 1994

Schneider, Russell. *Whatever Happened to Super Joe?* Gray & Company, 2006

Publications

Boston Herald
Chicago Tribune
Cleveland Indians 2017 Media Guide

Cleveland News
Cleveland Press
Cleveland Plain Dealer
Dallas Morning News
New York Times
The Sporting News
St. Louis Post-Dispatch

Websites

www.baseball-almanac.com
www.baseballhall.org
www.baseball-reference.com
www.basketball.reference.com
www.mlb.com/angels
www.mlb.com/orioles
www.mlb.com/tigers
www.mlb.com/whitesox
www.retrosheet.org
www.sabr.org
www.seamheads.com

Acknowledgments

For any article or book that is published, the author very often was given strong support to aid them in completing the finished manuscript. This was especially true in my case. Although the book that you now hold in your hands came from me and my keyboard, it was put through the editing wringer many times in order to present you with a fun, enjoyable, and hopefully informative volume.

First off, my thanks to my friend and colleague Rick Huhn. I have known Rick for over ten years and our friendship has been my good fortune. He steered this project in my direction last spring, and I will always be grateful. Rick also took the time to read through each question, and he offered sound advice and thoughtful critique in order to clean up the manuscript.

Thanks to Ken Samelson, Senior Editor at Skyhorse Publishing in New York City. Once Ken laid out the project and explained what his expectations of me were, it became a much more manageable process. He was very patient and answered any questions that I had, and he was supportive of my efforts from the onset.

D. Bruce Brown is the trivia maven and a member of the Society for American Baseball Research (SABR). Each year at the annual SABR convention, Bruce creates the individual and team trivia contests. It is easily one of the highlights of the week, and his questions test even the most knowledgeable baseball fans. I had requested that he supply me with questions regarding the Cleveland Indians, and he provided me with a plethora of them. Thank you, Bruce.

Most of the photos in the book are courtesy of the photo collection at the Cleveland Public Library. The staff was very helpful in pulling endless photo files for me to sift through on a single afternoon. I am appreciative of their assistance.

I am thankful to the fine authors and researchers at SABR. Although I knew most of the answers to the questions I had written, doing the research to write out the additional information that went with each answer was a huge task. I constantly referred to the Bio Project and the Games Project on the SABR website. The fine writing and research done by SABR members made my task so much easier.

It occurred to me that it might be a good idea to enlist a couple of Tribe fans to "test" their knowledge with regards to Indians baseball. My goal was to see how two lifelong Indians fans that are quite educated about the team's history, would do on the "test." I am thankful to Dale Rzonca and Jim Corrigan for taking the time to try and answer all 100 questions. This exercise proved to be a formidable task for both.